Advances in Business in Asia

Advances in Business in Asia:
The Opportunities, Threats, and Future Trends
of Businesses in China, India
and the ASEAN Countries

Edited by

Chris Perryer, Victor Egan and Brian Sheehan

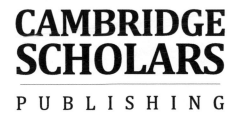

CAMBRIDGE
SCHOLARS
PUBLISHING

Advances in Business in Asia:
The Opportunities, Threats, and Future Trends of Businesses
in China, India and the ASEAN Countries,
Edited by Chris Perryer, Victor Egan and Brian Sheehan

This book first published 2012

Cambridge Scholars Publishing

12 Back Chapman Street, Newcastle upon Tyne, NE6 2XX, UK

British Library Cataloguing in Publication Data
A catalogue record for this book is available from the British Library

ISBN (10): 1-4438-3606-0, ISBN (13): 978-1-4438-3606-7

TABLE OF CONTENTS

PREFACE

The Asian Forum on Business Education (AFBE) was initially founded in Bangkok in 1992. It is a not-for-profit organisation that provides focus on business and business education in the Asia region by way of an online journal and annual conferences (see http://www.afbe.biz).

This book series represents selected papers from the conferences conducted by AFBE, which are co-hosted by universities in the various countries of the Asia region. Conferences pertain to a stated theme; the sub-title of this volume has been derived from the AFBE conference conducted in May 2010 in Bangkok, Thailand, and hosted by Mahasarakham University.

As readers will observe from the papers included, eminent academics have presented a broad array of issues associated with the opportunities and threats for business in China, India, and the member countries of the Association of South-East Asian Nations (ASEAN). The introduction draws together the diversity of issues by suggesting that global capitalism is itself threatened within the context of considerable future opportunities for entrepreneurial business activity, and also suggests that academia around the world has generally failed to adequately influence the debate.

We hope that readers will find interest in the topics covered, as well as reflect upon the dangers posed to the future of the macro-environment within which we all find ourselves indelibly embedded.

—Professor Dr Brian Sheehan
President
Asian Forum on Business Education

CHAPTER ONE

INTRODUCTION:
IN SEARCH OF A MIDDLE-PATH
FOR GLOBALISATION

VICTOR EGAN AND CHRIS PERRYER

China, India, and the ten member countries of the Association of South-East Asian Nations (ASEAN) (i.e., Singapore, Malaysia, Thailand, Indonesia, the Philippines, Vietnam, Laos, Cambodia, Brunei, and Myanmar) together account for about 40 percent of the world's population, and about 10 percent of global GDP. By the middle of the 21st-century, the outputs of China and India are expected to exceed those of the US and EU. What effect this shifting configuration will have on the world is merely speculative, but one thing is certain – the world will be very different in terms of economic and geo-political influences.

The emergence of China from 1978, and India since the 1980s, is strongly correlated to the globalisation of products and services that became the ubiquitous paradigm in global economics. It emerged post-World War II as world leaders sought to forge a new era of interaction based on cooperation, inclusiveness, and a less zero-sum approach. At the international level, the General Agreement on Tariffs and Trade (GATT) provided the basic parameters of interaction from 1947. GATT morphed into the World Trade Organization (WTO) in the 1990s, which then continued the work to foster trade liberalisation; the Doha Round being the most recent forum for trade negotiations.

The emergence of GATT at the international level highlighted the need for an apposite economic framework for nation-states. To this end, the eminent economist Paul Samuelson (1948) was the philosophical architect of the 'mixed economy' model of economic organisation. He imagined the role of government was to fill the gap in market failures, such as in the areas of inequality, public infrastructure, education, and the provision of macroeconomic stability. In other words, the progress of communities,

Samuelson contended, was dependent on a mix of free-market capitalism, moderated by appropriate government intervention.

The mixed economy paradigm was dominant until the global economic woes of the 1970s led to the rise of ultra-free-market libertarianism, harbouring the thesis that governments are incompetent and untrustworthy, and hence, should be excised from the provision of public goods. This view was academically assisted by small government advocates such as Frederick Hayek (1965) and Milton Friedman (1982), and put to practice in the 1980s by Ronald Reagan in the US and Margaret Thatcher in the UK.

After three decades of inexorable global capitalism, we are now confronted with a Manichean conundrum; "some remarkable successes, some disturbing failures, and a collection of what might best be called running sores" (Saul 2005, p.3). The 2008 Global Financial Crisis (GFC) is one such 'running sore' that furnishes insight into an international system that has disaggregated itself from communities; it demonstrates that the world has achieved a level of interconnectedness that now exceeds the reach of national economic policies and international architecture (Spence 2011).

What has become patently obvious from the GFC is that Paul Samuelson was, indeed, correct - markets fail; sometimes badly, and hence, require appropriate government intervention. Sach (2011) goes further in arguing that the GFC was not simply a short-term market failure, but rather a more fundamental enigma from several decades of moral decay in the social fabric of Western societies. The outcomes of this moral decay have been increasing inequality, ecological duress, and the marginalisation of citizenry. As Stiglitz (2010, p.295) notes, "the failures of our financial system are emblematic of broader failures in our economic system, and the failures of our economic system reflect deeper problems in our society". What Stiglitz (2010) alludes to is a fracturing of community that has led to the renunciation by the privileged and parvenu of all moral responsibility to the indigent, and indeed, to society as a whole (Homer-Dixon 2006; Sachs 2011). Chomsky (2011, p.5) reflects that "privilege yields opportunity, and opportunity confers responsibilities"; responsibilities that have been abrogated within a system devoted to profligate hedonism.

Perhaps the most insidious fiction perpetrated by global capitalism is the illusion that anyone is capable of becoming wealthy. But there is room at the top for merely a few, and few have the aptitude, intelligence, character, and/or luck to claim a place (Foley 2010). The recent 'occupations' of Wall Street, London, and Sydney, to name just several of the 'occupied' locations in over 80 countries around the world are indicative that a growing number of citizens are becoming wise to the fiction. Such 'occupations' are testament to an economic system that is heavily biased towards the "comfortably endowed" (Galbraith 1994, p.264), and in which the '99% majority' appear to benefit marginally at best. The 'occupy' movements are well cognisant that too many citizens have been subject to austerity programs and unemployment, while governments have provided bail-outs to financial institutions, and tax relief to the wealthy and powerful. To add further to the malignity of the 'occupiers', the term 'too big to fail' has worryingly gained currency in the contemporary economic and political lexicon – a dangerous dialogue, indeed, since it propels the idea that some corporations will only ever be permitted to win, irrespective of incompetent managerial decision-making or morally bankrupt behaviours.

Globalisation has also been stigmatised by graft and corruption, which serve to further bias a highly distorted economic system. An examination of Transparency International's Corruption Perception Index indicates that China, India, and the countries of ASEAN vary significantly in the ranking and scores of the perceived prevalence of corruption (TI 2011) [US included for comparison]:

Country	Rank	Score
Singapore	1	9.3
US	22	7.1
Brunei	38	5.5
Malaysia	56	4.4
China	78	3.5
Thailand	78	3.5
India	87	3.3
Indonesia	110	2.8
Vietnam	116	2.7
Philippines	134	2.4
Laos	154	2.1
Cambodia	154	2.1
Myanmar	176	1.4

Rank order, unfortunately, masks the real parlous state of global corruption. When viewed from the perspective of scores, it becomes apparent that only 2 countries out of the ASEAN 10 plus China and India score above 5.0; the point separating the 'highly clean' from the 'highly corrupt', and indicative of what Transparency International refers to as "a serious corruption problem" (TI 2011).

In response to the concatenating polemics of globalisation, Sachs (2011) calls for a "revitalisation of civic virtue" (p.x) by the corporate world, with a focus on the triple bottom-line of efficiency, fairness, and sustainability. Sachs (2011) also reminds us that the market economy is a sophisticated "human contrivance" (p.46), rather than a figment of evolution from the natural order. As such, the market economy requires continual intervention and innovation.

A dominant source of the theoretical framework for intervention and innovation might reasonably be expected to emanate from the academic world. However, along with abrogation of social responsibility by governments and powerful individuals under free-market libertarianism, business academia has also failed to provide the theoretical framework and moral compass so desperately needed, either because of collusion within the mainstream business milieu [those Chomsky (2011, p.5) refers to as "conformist intellectuals"], or more likely because of its emasculation by self-indulgent irrelevance to, and disconnect from, the real world of business and community. Business schools have become seduced in their quest for rankings, status, and enrolments (see, for example, Armstrong 2005; Augier & March 2007; Bennis & O'Toole 2005; Pfeffer & Fong 2002). Business academia has been complicit, described as an "incestuous, closed loop" (Hambrick 1994, 13) that maintains a quixotic compulsion to embrace certitude from contextually-isolated intellectual edifices (Currie et al. 2010; Gosling and Mintzberg 2006), and then fails to reach into the world of business practitioners for the dissemination of practical knowledge (Reed 2009); a pervasive example of what Saul (1992, p.575) insightfully refers to as the "folly of professional dialects".

Building on Kay's (2003, p.323) rather platonic observation that "capitalism should be replaced by something nicer", considerable socio-psychological dialogue has ensued in an attempt to resolve the societal decay succinctly observed by Sach (2011), Stiglitz (2010), Homer-Dixon (2006), and a plethora of others. The spiritual perspective of societal progress fosters the notion of moderation and a middle path by all stakeholders. The developments include 'spiritual capital' (Zohar & Marshall 2004), 'social economics' (O'Boyle 1999), 'Buddhist economics' (Schumaker 1973), and 'sufficiency economy' (Piboolsravut 2004).

Spiritual Capital

Zohar and Marshall (2004) offer 'spiritual capital' as an alternative to the darker side of market capitalism. They suggest focus on spiritual capital would provide the necessary transition from a purely profit, wealth, and power ideology, to include a sense of community, as well as humane values, such as honesty, trust, and responsibility.

Social Economics

Calvinism provided the religious undergirding for the economic libertarianism that has formed the basis of American life and the global economic system. The basic creed inculcates the idea that business and career success, materialism, and conspicuous consumption are divine signs that one is in favour with the Christian God. The corollary to this creed is that disdain should rightfully be heaped upon the indigent, since their situation is the axiomatic result of laziness, lack of motivation, and decadence (Klein 1985). In contrast to the doctrinal teachings of Christianity, the practical outcome of US-style Calvinist fundamentalism has been a withdrawal from the morality of caring, concern, and empathy for fellow citizens. Social economics prompts the view that the 'invisible hand' of the market does not protect the common good, nor does it lead to decent social outcomes for all citizens. An effective and sustainable economic system requires "the 'visible hand' of government to work with the 'invisible hand' of the markets" (Thanawala 2002, p.673).

Buddhist Economics

The Western ideology of social economics has its Eastern counterpart in, what Schumacher (1973, p.48) articulates as "Buddhist economics". Buddhist theology advocates a moderate 'middle path' between the sensual pleasure of egocentrism and self-mortifying asceticism. In the corporate environment, Buddhist economics focuses on developing employees to their full potential, creating team-orientedness, the satisfying of needs (rather than unconstrained wants), and respect, consideration, and honesty for all stakeholders (Holmes 1997; Schumacher 1973). By reinvigorating ethical and moral considerations in neoclassical Western economic thought, Buddhist economics aspires to achieve economic ends by constraining demand and managing supply (Alexandrin 1993).

Sufficiency Economy

Buddhist economics is the socio-religious underpinning of Thailand's 'sufficiency economy' philosophy. The message delivered in a speech by His Majesty King Bhumibol Adulyadej in 1974 was reiterated following Thailand's economic crisis in 1997, and later encapsulated in the definition

provided by the National Economic and Social Development Board
(NESDB) of Thailand in 1999:

> " 'Sufficiency Economy' is a philosophy that stresses *the middle path* as
> an overriding principle for appropriate conduct by the populace at all
> levels. This applies to conduct starting from the level of the families,
> communities, as well as the level of nation in development and
> administration so as to modernise in line with the forces of globalisation.
> 'Sufficiency' means moderation, reasonableness, and the need of self-
> immunity mechanism for sufficient protection from impact arising from
> internal and external changes. To achieve this, an application of
> knowledge with due consideration and prudence is essential. In particular,
> great care is needed in the utilization of theories and methodologies for
> planning and implementation in every step. At the same time, it is essential
> to strengthen the moral fibre of the nation, so that everyone, particularly
> political and public officials, academics, businessmen at all levels, adhere
> first and foremost to the principle of honesty and integrity. In addition, a
> way of life based on patience, perseverance, diligence, wisdom, and
> prudence is indispensable to create balance and be able to cope
> appropriately with critical challenges arising from extensive and rapid
> socioeconomic, environmental, and cultural changes in the world"
> (NESDB 1999, cited in Piboolsravut 2004, p.128).

In essence, then, sufficiency economy entails moderation of needs,
mutual reliance and cooperation, harmony between economic activities
and the environment, and self-immunity from exogenous shocks (He
2006). The philosophy is based on a middle path between the needs of
community and individuals, and between markets and the environment. In
practical terms, individuals are advised to avoid excessive consumption
and focus on basic needs, corporate enterprises should avoid over-
expansion and focus on productivity, and government intervention should
focus on the protection of community and environment (Crispin 2006).

For corporations and individuals, the opportunities in the Asia region
over the coming years are considerable, but so too are the challenges and
threats. Globalisation, as an economic theory, is presently at risk of
becoming a sclerotic artefact of an era in which political leaders and
citizens became beguiled by the illusion of prosperity for all. Reflective
analysis of thirty years of globalisation now attests to an awkward truth of
persistent discontent and conflict, pollution and climate change, and the
cold realisation that wealth and power are the preserve of a few. On the
other hand, the main benefit of the economic system for citizens has
devolved into meretricious consumerism in the constant search for
perfunctory happiness; the "enchantment of imminence", as described by
Foley (2010, p.34). There was surely something inordinately simplistic,

and even absurd, in the belief that individual greed and self-interest could be harnessed for the common good without consequence to community.

Economists remain divided on whether more or less government control is the way forward (Homer-Dixon 2006); politicians align according to ideological bents; and uncertainty prevails for all as to how the economic system should reform. But uncertainty leads to choice, and choice means opportunity – opportunity to resolve the 'disturbing failures' and 'running sores' that continue to grow in scale and scope.

As a means of resolution, we contend that there is dire need for a middle-path; for moderation; for equilibrium, whether by a "revitalisation of civic virtue" (Sach 2001, p.x); a rebirth of 'spiritual capital' (Zohar & Marshall 2004), or a shift towards 'social economics' (O'Boyle 1999), 'Buddhist economics' (Schumaker 1973), or 'sufficiency economy' (Piboolsravut 2004). There is far too much at stake to ignore the increasing cadre of marginalised citizenry, and continue abated on the same market fundamentalist course as has been the case since the 1980s.

The dialogue thus far has furnished thoughts and provocations on the promised opportunities and ensuing threats of global capitalism. The papers in the current volume have been included to provide more specific insights into issues that impact on business in China, India, and the member countries of ASEAN.

T. Prasanna provides an insight into the impact of the WTO's General Agreement on Trade in Services (GATS) on foreign direct investment in India since 1995. He outlines many of the expected longer-term benefits for India, such as employment opportunities and technology transfer, and annunciates inhibiting factors with which the Indian government must grapple in order to achieve the full realisation of those benefits. Prasanna's paper points to the significance of government to the well-being of economies. However, in the case of India, it is more about moderating the bureaucracy than extending the reach of government bureaucrats.

Kanitsorn Terdaopong and Yang Yin expose issues associated with small and medium size enterprises (SMEs) in China, finding a propensity in Chinese SMEs for short-term debt, rather than long-term debt so common in Western companies. Additionally, and perhaps understandably, they found that unhealthy Chinese SMEs were characterised by excessive short-term debt, which leaves them highly vulnerable in times of economic downturn.

Paul Hughes provides an insightful case study of the process to establish an international joint venture (IJV) start-up involving an American entrepreneur, Thai operators, and Indian analysts. Issues with IJVs are particularly salient to global capitalism due to both their proliferation, and their problems. For example, studies suggest that perhaps 30-70 percent of IJVs perform somewhere between unsatisfactory and complete failure (Buttery & Buttery 1994; Killing 1983). Moreover, IJVs can also provide an inhibition to company growth. For example, Sony and Ericsson recently dissolved their IJV for the manufacture of mobile phones with Sony acquiring Ericsson's 50 percent stake. Sony perceived a strategic advantage in gaining full control, and hence, the ability to integrate the mobile phone business with its other products, thus enhancing operational efficiencies in engineering, network development, and marketing (Virki 2011).

Mark Speece, Jonathan Lee, and Jun Han explore the machinations of *guanxi* in China. Indeed, Asian economic growth since the 1950s has been largely built on such relational networks that have provided the basic institutional medium for political, social, and economic activities (Hamilton 1996; Pyatt et al. 2001; Yen 2002). Lee et al. (2001) identified three different types of Chinese *guanxi* relationships:

- *Expressive ties*: Relationships that are permanent and stable, personal and affective; applies to family, relatives, and old friends.
- *Instrumental ties*: Relationships that are temporary and unstable, impersonal and utilitarian; applies to unknown others.
- *Mixed ties*: Relationships that are somewhat permanent and stable, but are elastic and may change; characteristic of general business linkages; based on reciprocity of favours or *renqing*, and the social regulatory mechanism of 'losing face'.

Another relational principle characteristic of the Chinese in South-east Asia is the formation of close ties with local politically-influential elites; referred to as 'pariah entrepreneurship' (Riggs 1966), 'ersatz capitalism' (Yoshihara 1988), and 'the dark side' of Asian business (Backman 1999). For example, the Board of Directors of the Kuok Group (the most successful firm in Malaysia by the 1990s) included a judicious array of aristocrats, military generals, and senior public servants (Heng 1993). Likewise, the rise of the Bangkok Bank in Thailand from the 1950s can be directly correlated with the early involvement of military generals and senior bureaucrats as Board members and executives (Mackie 1993). In a similar vein, Robison (1993) describes the networks of patronage evident in Indonesia, which involve bureaucrats and Chinese-owned corporate groups, and which have led to monopolies, corruption, and market distortions.

In other words, *guanxi* has always been a vague concept, built more on pragmatism than strict adherence to social mores. Speece, Lee and Jun conclude similarly; in their case study, good customer service was the precursor to the development of *guanxi*, rather than the other way around.

Chris Perryer, Geoffrey Soutar, and Catherine Jordan researched ethical attitudes of Western tertiary educated people in seven countries, including Singapore, Indonesia, China, the Philippines, Australia, the US, and the UK. They examined two specific ethical attitudes: (1) self-advancement at the expense of co-workers; and, (2) misuse of organisational assets. Their findings indicate considerable differences across the countries, and pose as many questions as they provide answers. While the US, the UK, Singapore and China were relatively close on perceptions about the ethicality of personal advancement at the expense of co-workers, with China and Indonesia closely behind, the Philippines sample suggested that this posed much less an ethical problem. The US, UK, and China samples had similar attitudes to the ethicality of misusing organisational assets, with Singapore more relaxed, Australia even more relaxed, and the Philippines again seeing little by way of ethical hindrance. The surprise on this dimension was Indonesia, with that sample indicating very strong ethical attitudes. Perryer, Soutar, and Jordan argue that this may be an artefact of the common Western education of the sample, and discuss the implications for theory and practice.

Victor Egan's paper on recessionary effects and business constraints on small firms in Vietnam highlights the threat posed to heavily interconnected economies in times of global recession; a perversity of global capitalism that punishes nation-states merely for being part of the system. Egan found that the 2008 GFC effected retail sales by an average decline of 32 percent across the respondent companies. In addition, business constraints, including strong competition, high government taxes, poor infrastructure, and lack of skills of both employees and owners, were reported as hindrances to business efficiency in Vietnam.

Ma'Mum Sarma and Marthin Nanere present a paper comparing conventional and Sharia banks in Indonesia. Sharia banks have been of growing significance in Islamic countries in general, and rapidly growing in Indonesia since 1992, representing a more ethical alternative to the conventional Western model, which the GFC exposed as fickle and malignant. Sharia banks provide a degree of internalised regulation by promoting religious values as a mechanism to counter the dark side of global capitalism.

Rachaya Indanon provides a case study involving rice farmers in Thailand, noting the responsibility of the Thai government for positive intervention particularly in times of economic hardship. The paper reinforces the critical part played by the 'visible hand' of government in tempering the hardship of disadvantaged citizens.

Finally, Jitisa Roenjun and Mark Speece review the role of religiosity for Thai women in small business. The women were followers of the Buddhist reform movement, *Kuan Im Bodhisattva*. The authors found positive outcomes from a religious teaching based on gender equality. The women used Buddhist values in practice, closely approximating the application of the 'sufficiency economy' philosophy of living.

References

Alexandrin, G. 1993. Elements of Buddhist economics. *International Journal of Social Economics*. 20(2):3-11

Armstrong, S. 2005. Postgraduate management education in the UK: Lessons from or lessons for the U.S. model? *Academy of Management Learning & Education*. 4(2):229-234

Augier, M. & March, J.G. 2007. The pursuit of relevance in management education. *California Management Review*. 49(2):129-146

Backman, M. 1999. *Asian Eclipse: Exposing the Dark Side of Business in Asia*. Singapore: John Wiley

Bennis, W.G. & O'Toole, J. 2005. How business schools lost their way. *Harvard Business Review*. May:96-104

Buttery, E. & Buttery, A. 1994. *Business Networks*. Melbourne: Longman

Chomsky, N. 2011. The Responsibility of Intellectuals. *Boston Review*. September/October. Retrieved 9 November 2011 from http://www.bostonreview.net

Crispin, S.W. 2006. In Thailand, a return to 'sufficiency'. *Asia Times Online*. Retrieved November 30, 2006 from http://www.atimes.com/atimes/

Currie, G., Knights, D. & Starkey, K. 2010. Introduction: A post-crisis critical reflection on business schools. *British Journal of Management*. 21(1):S1-S5

Friedman, M. 1982. *Capitalism and Freedom*. London: Phoenix

Foley, M. 2010. *The Age of Absurdity*. London: Simon & Schuster

Galbraith, J.K. 1994. *The World Economy since the Wars*. London: Mandarin

Gosling, J. & Mintzberg, H. 2006. Management education as if both matter. *Management Learning*. 37(4):419-428

Hambrick, D.C. 1994. What if the academy actually mattered? *Academy of Management Review*. 19(1):11-16

Hamilton, G.G. 1996. The theoretical significance of Asian business networks. In G.G. Hamilton (ed.). *Asian Business Networks*. Berlin: Walter de Gruyter. 283-298

Heng, P.K. 1993. The Chinese business elite of Malaysia. in R. McVey (ed.). *Southeast Asian Capitalists*. New York: Cornell University. 127-144

Hayek, F.A. 1965. *The Road to Serfdom*. London: Phoenix

He, C. 2006. Speech delivered at the 'International workshop on sufficiency economy: Poverty reduction and the Millennium Development Goals to commemorate the 60th anniversary of His Majesty the King of Thailand's accession to the throne. July 27, 2006. Retrieved November 30, 2006 from
http://www.fao.org/world/regional/rap/speeches/2006/20060726.html

Holmes, D. 1997. *The Heart of Theravada Buddhism: The Noble Eightfold Path*. Bangkok: Chulalongkorn University

Homer-Dixon, T. 2006. *The Upside of Down*. Melbourne: Text

Kay, J. 2003. *The Truth about Markets: Why Some Nations are Rich, But Most Remain Poor*. London: Allen Lane

Killing, J.P. 1983. *Strategies for Joint Venture Success*. New York: Praeger

Klein, S. 1985. Two views of business ethics: A popular philosophical approach and a value based interdisciplinary one. *Journal of Business Ethics*. 4:71-79

Lee, D.-J., Pae, J.H. & Wong, Y.H. 2001. A model of close business relationships in China (guanxi). *European Journal of Marketing*. 35(1/2)

Mackie, J. 1993. Changing patterns of Chinese big business in Southeast Asia. in R. McVey (ed.). *Southeast Asian Capitalists*. New York: Cornell University. 161-190

O'Boyle, E.J. 1999. The nature of social economics: A personal commentary. *International Journal of Social Economics*. 26(1):46-55

Pfeffer, J. & Fong, C.T. 2002. The end of business schools? Less success than meets the eye. *Academy of Management Learning & Education*. 1(1):78-95.

Piboolsravut, P. 2004. Sufficiency Economy. *ASEAN Economic Bulletin*. 21(1):127-134

Pyatt, R., Ashkanasy, N.M., Tamaschke, R. & Grigg, T. 2001. Transitions and traditions in Chinese family businesses: Evidence from Hong Kong and Thailand. in J.B. Kidd, X. Li & F.-J. Richter (eds.). *Advances in Human Resource Management in Asia*. Basingstoke: Palgrave. 80-104

Reed, M.I. 2009. The theory/practice gap: A problem for research in business schools? *Journal of Management Development*. 28(8):685-693.

Riggs, F. 1966. *Thailand: The Modernization of a Bureaucratic Polity*. Honolulu: University of Hawaii

Robison, R. 1993. Industrialization and the economic and political development of capital: The case of Indonesia. in R. McVey (ed.). *Southeast Asian Capitalists*. New York: Cornell. 66-88

Sachs, J. 2011. *The Price of Civilization*. London: Bodley Head.

Samuelson, P. 1948. *Economics*. New York: McGraw-Hill.

Saul, J.R. 1992. *Voltaire's Bastards: The Dictatorship of Reason in the West*. London: Sinclair-Stevenson.

—. 2005. *The Collapse of Globalism and the Reinvention of the World*. London: Penguin.

Schumacher, E.F. 1973. *Small is Beautiful: A Study of Economics as if People Mattered*. London: Blond & Briggs

Spence, M. 2011. *The Next Convergence: The Future of Economic Growth in a Multispeed World*. Perth: University of Western Australia.

Stiglitz, J. 2010. *Freefall: Free Markets and the Sinking of the Global Economy*. London: Allen Lane.

Thanawala, K. 2002. Reflections on private market economy and social market economy. *International Journal of Social Economics*. 29(7/8):663-674

TI 2011. *Corruption Perception Index 2010*. Transparency International. Retrieved 30 October 2011 from http://www.transparency.org

Virki, T. 2011. Sony buys Ericsson out of mobile phone venture. *Reuters*. 27 October. Retrieved October 30, 2011 from http://www.reuters.com

Yen, C.-H. 2002. *The Ethnic Chinese in East and Southeast Asia*. Singapore: Times Academic

Yoshihara, K. 1988. *The Rise of Ersatz Capitalism in South-East Asia*. Manila: Ateneo de Manila University

Zohar, D. & Marshall, I. 2004. *Spiritual Capital: Wealth We Can Live By*. London: Bloomsbury

CHAPTER TWO

IMPACT OF THE GENERAL AGREEMENT ON TRADE IN SERVICES (GATS) ON FOREIGN DIRECT INVESTMENT (FDI) IN SERVICES IN INDIA

T. PRASANNA

Abstract

The four key items on the agenda for the Hong Kong ministerial meetings in 2005 were services, agriculture, Non-Agricultural Market Access (NAMA), and differential treatment for developing countries. The draft of the Hong Kong declaration agreed on 18 December 2005 speaks about further liberalization in Mode 3; that is, the `commercial presence' category of service providers. This will usher in increased Foreign Direct Investment (FDI) in a vast gamut of service sectors, such as banking, insurance, construction, engineering, tourism, education, telecommunication, and computer-related and professional services. It also provides for removal or substantial reduction of economic needs tests, such as relaxing the norm that local employment should be generated. India should utilize the opportunity the liberalization has provided, in attracting the FDI in services sectors to the optimum, and maintain regulation aimed at economic growth.

Introduction

The presence of efficient services in infrastructure is a precondition for economic success. Services, such as telecommunications, transport, banking, and insurance, supply strategically important inputs to all other sectors of the economy. The global economy is gradually becoming dominated by the service sector. The importance of this sector can be judged by the fact that world trade in commercial services amounted to

US$1,440bn in 2001, which is equal to 23 percent of goods trade. The sector represented well over 60 percent of global GDP by 2006. In India, during 2006-7 the service sector accounted for 55.1 percent of the country's GDP, and provided employment for 26 percent of the total workforce, while industry, which had a share of 26.4 percent of GDP, employed 22 percent. About 52 percent of the Indian workforce is employed in the farming sector, which contributes 18.5 percent of GDP.

Most of the rapid growth in the service sector is attributed to the growth in information technology and business process outsourcing services. However, telecommunications, the financial sector, and the tourism and travel industry have also shown a rapidly increasing growth curve. Considering that services accounted for 5 percent of global trade at US$1.54tn in 2002, the services sector will play an increasingly significant role in India's economic development.

Since 2004, India's share of global trade has increased significantly. According to trade statistics published by the World Trade Organization (WTO), India's share in total world trade (which includes trade in merchandise, services, and agricultural produce) has increased from 1.1 percent in 2004 (i.e., the initial year of the new Foreign Trade Policy 2004-09) to 1.5 percent in 2006. The WTO statistics show that India has emerged as one of the dynamic suppliers of services in the world, and in 2010 was ranked 21st in export of services and 27th in service imports. India software exports account for 48 percent of total service exports (NASSCOM). However, the need to move faster assumes greater importance, considering that countries like Hong Kong, Singapore, and the South Korea have a share of 2.9 percent, 1.8 percent, and 1.9 percent respectively in global services trade.

The service sector has also played an important role in attracting foreign capital, with key producer services accounting for a growing share of FDI inflows into the Indian economy. Given the service sector's role in facilitating India's interconnectedness with the global economy, the WTO's General Agreement on Trade in Services (GATS) has high significance for India. GATS provides India with a framework to liberalize services trade in modes and activities where it has a comparative advantage. India's main source of comparative advantage in services is its labour endowment. The country has the potential to export labour-intensive services at all skill levels, through cross-border movement of service providers (i.e., mode 4 of GATS).

The Indian economy, since 1991, has opened her door in a systematic way to global capitalist forces. This has its impact on all sectors. FDI flows have increased enormously to India. FDI involves the transfer of financial capital, technology, and other skills to the host country, and contributes to entrepreneurship, and managerial, professional, and technical expertise (Brewer 1989). The host economy benefits from the additional economic activity, creating employment and tax revenue. Entry by foreign firms can also increase competition in domestic markets, reduce monopoly profits, and stimulate quality upgrades of products and services by all firms in the sector. FDI also stimulates economic growth, and often has a larger impact than domestic investment.

Objectives

The objective of this paper is, with respect to India:
- To analyze the progress of the pattern of growth of FDI in service sectors;
- To estimate the prospects of growth of FDI in service sectors;
- To identity the sector which is attracting more FDI;
- To suggest policies for increasing FDI flows; and,
- To identify the factors that hinder growth in service sectors.

GATS is playing a crucial role in stimulating trade and development by seeking to create a predictable policy environment wherein the member countries voluntarily undertake to bind their policy-regimes relating to trade in services. GATS came into existence as a result of the Uruguay Round of negotiations and entered into force on 1 January 1995, with the establishment of the WTO. The main purpose for the creation of GATS was to create a credible and reliable system of international trade rules, which ensure fair and equitable treatment of all countries on the principles of non-discrimination.

The growth of trade in services is expected to lead to the following benefits which will increase the economic performance of India and other countries:
- **Greasing the wheels of Development**
The access to world-class services in developing countries helps exporters and producers to capitalize on their competitive strength in the goods and services they are selling.
- **Employment Opportunities**
The growth in trade in services promotes employment within the country so as to absorb disguised unemployment from agriculture. There will also be wide opportunities for professionals to work internationally.

- **Consumer Choice**

Consumers, in a real sense, will be 'kings' as they receive a variety of choices with better quality. The competition will lower prices and provide wider choices for consumers.

- **Technology Transfer**

Services liberalization encourages FDI flow into the economy. Such FDI generally brings with it new skills and technologies that spill over into the wider economy in various ways.

The WTO Secretariat has divided services into 12 sectors (which are subsequently divided into 161 sub-sectors): (1) Business (including professional and computer services); (2) Communication; (3) Construction and engineering; (4) Distribution (e.g., commission agents, wholesale and retail trade and franchising); (5) Education; (6) Environment; (7) Finance (including insurance and banking); (8) Health; (9) Tourism and travel; (10) Recreation, cultural and sporting; (11) Transportation; and, (12) Other services not elsewhere classified.

Modes of GATS

GATS provides for four modes of supply of services: (1) Cross-border; (2) Consumption abroad; (3) Commercial presence; and, (4) Presence/movement of natural persons.

Mode 1

Cross-border supply refers to a situation where the service flows from the territory of one member country into the territory of another. For example, an architect can send his architectural plan through electronic means; a teacher can send teaching material to students in any other country; a doctor sitting in India can advise his patient in the US through electronic means. In all these cases, trade in services takes place and this is equivalent to cross-border movement of goods.

Mode 2

Consumption abroad refers to a situation where a consumer of a service moves into the territory of another member country to obtain the service. For example, tourists utilising hotel or restaurant services abroad; ship or aircraft repairs or maintenance services abroad.

Mode 3
Commercial presence implies that service suppliers from a member country establish a territorial presence in another member country with a view to providing services. In this case, the service supplier establishes a legal presence in the form of a joint venture/subsidiary/representative branch office in the host country and supplies services.

Mode 4
Presence or movement of natural persons (i.e., export of manpower) covers situations in which a service is delivered through persons of a member country temporarily entering the territory of another member country. Examples include independent service suppliers (for example, doctors, engineers, consultants, and accountants). However, GATS covers only temporary movement and not citizenship, residence, or employment on a permanent basis in a foreign country.

The GATS Agreement enforces two types of general obligations on the part of the signatories:
- **Most Favoured Nation Treatment:** Under the MFN treatment a country is obliged to provide a treatment to a country, which is no less favorable than the treatment it provides to any other country (i.e., if a GATS member country offers certain privilege to any other country, whether it be a member or not, it has to extend the same treatment to all GATS member countries). However, GATS allows member countries to undertake exemptions to this clause, in initial commitments, subject to review.
- **Transparency:** This clause requires every country to publish all measures of general applications that affect the operation of the Agreement. This clause is extremely important for traders doing business in a foreign country, as they are often not aware of the laws and regulations of the other country.

India as a Destination for FDI

There are a number of reasons cited as important for India becoming an important FDI destination: (1) A middle-class of 350 million and over 1 billion consumers as a whole; (2) India is located between central Asia and south-east Asia with huge markets; (3) Labour is relatively cheap; (4) Strong technical manpower that can be hired cheaply; (5) Unexploited abundant natural resources; (6) Determination of the government to carry forward the economic reforms; and, (7) India has the second largest

English speaking scientific and technical manpower resource base in the world.

Hence, there is vast scope for increase in FDI in services in India. The service sectors play a crucial role in generating employment. The top five biggest job creators in India are (Malini Goyal 2006); (1) IT and ITES; (2) Banking and finance; (3) Retail; (4) Hospitality and travel; and, (5) Telecommunications.

FDI Ownership Caps

Indian FDI laws have taken a more liberal approach by specifying 'a negative list' of sectors with limited levels of FDI. Very few sectors (e.g., agriculture) completely prohibit foreign ownership. The Indian government has even opened the defense industry to limited foreign participation. Many sectors allow 100 percent foreign ownership, including software, non-bank corporations, roads, general manufacturing, pharmaceuticals, airports, tourism/hotels, and courier services. Other sectors allow between 26 percent and 74 percent foreign ownership. The government is gradually liberalizing the FDI regime, recently increasing FDI limits on defense, telecommunications, and insurance. Table 1 shows the FDI regimes across the various services sectors.

If we compare the openness in Indian policy, in terms of the sphere of operations, with the policies of major competing countries, we find that in China FDI is encouraged in manufacturing and agricultural activities. Another country that has opened agriculture to FDI is Thailand. However, FDI is not permitted in agriculture and mining in many other competing Asian countries. Generally, manufacturing industries are open to FDI in all countries in Asia. In the case of service industries, there are wide variations. In China, all service industries (except hotels) are closed to foreign investment. On the other hand, in Thailand, FDI is permitted in almost all service industries. India, like most other Asian countries, stays in between the two extreme policy stances.

The most striking feature of the present liberalization policy in India is the freedom provided to the level of foreign equity participation. In the earlier policy phases, the attitude was quite rigid with respect to foreign equity ownership and control. It was insisted that FDI should be accompanied by technology transfer agreements. In addition, foreign ownership exceeding 40 percent of equity was granted only in exceptional cases. In striking contrast, under the liberalization policy, it is now not necessary that FDI is accompanied by foreign technology agreements.

Moreover, FDI is given automatic approval up to 51 percent foreign equity in the listed priority industries, which cover most manufacturing activities, including software development and those related to hotels and tourism. Besides, there is no upper bound limit for foreign equity, even 100 percent foreign equity is permitted with prior approval. Permission is given freely to 100 percent foreign equity in the power sector, and wholly export-oriented industries, all manufacturing activities in special the economic zone in the telecommunication sector for internet service providers, infrastructure providers, and electronic mail and voice mail. Further, the government has developed a liberal approach towards non-resident Indian (NRI) investment: NRIs and overseas corporate bodies (OCBs) can invest up to 100 percent in the real estate sector and in certain other high priority industries. Clearly, the change in the government's attitude is basic in the sense that FDI is also looked to as a channel of financial resources for investment independent of foreign technology transfer and foreign majority equity. Hence, foreign control is freely allowed to attract FDI inflows into priority industries.

South Korea is the only other country, where an automatic approval system exists, though it is confined to minority interests under certain conditions. South Korea has a well-defined regulation governing FDI and its "negative list system" with prohibited and restricted sectors, reflects the stability and transparency so important to an attractive FDI policy.

By 2007, India had emerged as the second most-attractive location for global FDI; next only to China, and ahead of the US and Russia. There was a three-fold increase in FDI inflows during 2006-07 over the previous year. FDI inflows reached US$6.6bn as against US$3.7bn over the corresponding period the year prior, reflecting the continuing pace of expansion of domestic activities, a positive investment climate, and a long-term view of India as an investment destination. The services sector was in the forefront accounting for 34.2 percent of the total inflows during this period, followed by the construction industry with a share of 20.6 percent. While Mauritius continued to be the dominant source of FDI to India, Singapore replaced the US as the next important source. Table 2 shows yearly FDI inflows to India between 1991 and 2006.

Table 1: Maximum Foreign Ownership

Service Sector	Maximum foreign ownership
Mining and exploration	100% all ventures, except diamonds where the limit is 74%, and coal which is reserved for public sector and captive private mines
Advertising and films	100% films; 74% advertising
Ports	100% BOT projects; 74% non-BOT Projects
Professional (except legal)	51%
Automobiles	51%
Banking	74%
Non-banking financial	51-74%
Telecommunications	49-74%
Petroleum refining	26% public enterprises; 49% domestic private companies
Insurance	26%
Defense	26%
Real estate	0% except for 100% in townships, resorts, hotels, housing and commercial premises.
Print media	0% print media; 20% broadcasting; 49% non-resident Indian investment
Agriculture	0%
E-commerce; internet	100%
Airport	74%
Manufacturing	100%
Insurance	26%
Mass rapid transport	100%
Pharmaceuticals	100%
Courier	100%

Table 2: Yearly FDI Inflows: 1991-2006

Year	Amount FDI Inflows	
	Rupees million	US$ million
1991-1992	409	167
1992-1993	1,094	393
1993-1994	2,018	654
1994-1995	4,312	1,374
1995-1996	6,916	2,141
1996-1997	9,654	2,770
1997-1998	13,548	3,682
1998-1999	12,343	3,083
1999-2000	10,311	2,439
2000-2001	12,645	2,908
2001-2002	19,361	4,222
2002-2003	14,932	3,134
2003-2004	12,117	2,634
2004-2005	17,138	3,755
2005-2006	34,316	7,751
Total	**171,114**	**41,107**

Source: Compiled from relevant years Indian Economic Survey

Table 3 demonstrates the important sectors which received more FDI flows between 1991 and 2006 were business services that received 16.2 percent, followed by the transportation industry which received 10.19 percent, financial and non-financial services which received 9.52 percent, and telecommunications which received 9.38 percent. Others included food processing, pharmaceuticals, consultancy, engineering, textiles, and tourism.

Banking
As at 2011, there were 27 public sector banks in India, and entry of foreign banks remained highly regulated. State-owned banks control 80 percent of the banking system. The Reserve Bank of India has granted operating approval to 25 new foreign banks, or bank branches, since liberalization by issuing new guidelines in 1993. As of September 2004, 35 foreign banks with 217 branches were operating in India. Five US banks now have a total of 16 branches in India. They operate under restrictive conditions including tight limitations on their ability to add sub-

branches. FDI in banking is slowly being liberalized, and the foreign equity ceiling has been raised to 74 percent from 49 percent for investment in private banks. FDI in state-owned banks remains capped at 20 percent. Foreign investor voting rights are capped at 10 percent in private banks and 1 percent in state-owned banks Foreign banks may operate in India through only one of three channels; branches, wholly owned subsidiary, or up to 74 percent ownership in a private Indian bank.

Table 3: Sectorial FDI Inflows: 1991-2006

Service Sector	Percent FDI inflows
Business	16.2%
Transportation	10.2%
Financial and non-financial	9.5%
Telecommunications	9.4%
Food Processing	3.6%
Pharmaceuticals	3.2%
Consultancy	1.6%
Engineering	1.5%
Textiles	1.3%
Trading	1.1%
Tourism	1.1%
Other	41.3%

Source: Relevant Issues of SIA Newsletter, Ministry of Industries and Commerce

Audiovisual and Communications Services

The Indian government has removed all the barriers to the import of motion pictures, although US companies have experienced difficulty in importing the film/video publicity materials and are unable to license movie-related merchandize due to royalty remittance restrictions. The legislation by the parliament passed in December 2002 allows the Indian government to put in place the Conditional Access System (CAS) for cable television whereby television subscribers would be required to install set-top-box decoders to view premium channels. In March 2004, in the face of considerable distributor and consumer resistance, as well as confusion surrounding pricing issues and other rules, the government suspended implementation of CAS pending review by a regulatory authority. The government permits FDI of up to 49 percent in Indian cable networks and companies that uplink from India. Total FDI in direct-to-home (DTH) broadcasting has been restricted to 49 percent, with an FDI ceiling of 20 percent on investments by broadcasting companies and cable companies. At present, news channels are permitted to have up to 26 percent foreign equity investment. As of August 2003, they must also ensure that a dominant Indian partner holds at least 51 percent equity. In addition, operational control of the editorial content must be in Indian hands.

Construction, Architecture and Engineering

Many construction projects are offered only on a non-convertible rupee payment basis. Only government projects financed by international development agencies permit payments in foreign currency. Foreign construction firms are not awarded government contracts unless local firms are unable to perform the work. Foreign firms may only participate through international joint ventures (IJVs) with Indian firms.

Telecommunications

India has one of the fastest growing telecommunications markets in the world, and has taken positive steps towards liberalizing the market and introducing private investment and competition in basic telecommunications services. The national telecommunications policy allows private participation in the provision of basic (including cellular) and value-added telecommunications services. Foreign equity in value added services is limited to 51 percent. For basic services, the limit was 49 percent, but was raised to 74 percent in February 2005. Private operators can provide services within regional 'circles' that roughly correspond to the borders of India's states. The government holds a 26 percent position in the international carrier VSNL, a 56 percent position in MTNL, which primarily serves the Delhi and Bombay metropolitan areas, and a 100 percent position in BSNL, which provides domestic services throughout the rest of India.

Retail and Distribution Services

The Indian distribution services sector is still very much in its infancy. In other similar countries, retailing contributes 14-20 percent of total workforce employment; in India, it is only 6-7 percent. One of the reasons for the lower contribution of this sector to GDP is that it is disorganized and highly fragmented with the majority of outlets having very low profit margins. A survey by the research group ORG found that in 19 consumer goods categories, 1,378 brands, and 2,579 individual products entered the

Indian market between 1990 and 1996. Over the past decade, India has strengthened its position as a sourcing hub for many large international apparel and home-furnishing retailers (for example, Pottery Barn, Crate and Barrel, Gap, and Ralph Lauren). In February 2002, Wal-Mart, the world's largest retailer, opened a global sourcing office in Bangalore to facilitate the sourcing of products from India.

The present policy is not allowing FDI in retail, while franchises are allowed to set up businesses on a case-by-case basis; many foreign retailers (for example, McDonald's, Nike, Levi's, Domino's) have entered the Indian market through this route. As compared to other services sectors, such as IT and education, the penetration of franchising in retailing and its success rate is much lower. The largest Indian retailer, Food World, had total sales of US$30m in 2010. This is less than one-sixth of the sale of a single Carrefour hypermarket.

Other Services

FDI is not permitted in the real estate sector. Construction sector growth is, therefore, restricted because of complex tenancy laws, rent control, high stamp duties, and poor enforcement of building regulations. Issues like minimum acreage development (100acres), minimum capitalization requirements (US$10m), and a 3-year lock-in period before repatriation of proceeds limit the attractiveness of this sector to foreign firms.

There is no cap on FDI in the health sector, but foreign individuals are prohibited from providing services for profit, and are subject to the registration requirements of the respective medical associations in India.

Professional services like accountancy, legal, postal, and rail transport are closed to foreign participation. The Bar Council, and the foreign services provider, must belong to a company which allows Indian nationals to practice in their country. FDI is not permitted in this sector, and international law firms are not authorized to open offices in India.

India's Future Markets

India has submitted 'requests' to trading partners for services in computer-related activities, architecture, health, audio-visual, tourism, maritime, and finance. A brief sector-wise description of the requests that India has made to its trading partners, as well as the ones it has received from them, are available at the web-site of the Department of Commerce. India circulated its initial offer in ongoing services negotiations under GATS in January 2004.

Barriers to Foreign Service Providers

A sector-wise analysis shows India has to liberalize many sectors. The following are some of the inhibiting factors:

- In few sectors though GATS commitment is to allow FDI of 51 percent. India has liberalized up to 100 percent through the automatic route with the exception of B2B (Business to Business) electronic commerce where FIPB approval is required and foreign promoters are required to disinvest 26 percent of ownership;
- Lack of government will in developing labour laws;
- Excessive bureaucratic regulation;
- Poor quality Infrastructure; and,
- The Indian government continues to prohibit or severely restrict FDI in politically sensitive sectors, such as agriculture, retail trade, rail, and real estate.

Sustainability of the Service Sector in India

India has one of the largest road networks in the world, aggregating approximately 3.31 million kilometres. National highways constitute over 65 million kilometres. India has the second largest telecom network in the world, as measured in terms of the number of phones. There are over 296 million cellular subscribers in the country, and the cellular customer base is growing at a rate of approximately 8 to 10 million per month. As a result, the tele-density had risen to 30. Tele-density (number of telephones per 100 people) is an indicator of the expansion of telecommunication services in the country. However, India's tele-density is still far below that of China (43), the US (116), Australia (123), and the UK (143), suggesting a great deal of scope for further expansion.

The introduction of competition in the telecom sector has led to a dramatic drop in tariffs. In particular, GSM tariffs had dropped from Rs14.5/min in 1998 to Rs0.50/min in 2004. National and international long distance rates have also dropped dramatically with the shift away from a monopolistic market to a more competitive one.
http://www.neoncarrot.co.uk/h_aboutindia/india_economy_stats.html - outsourcing_IT

Conclusions

The four key items on the agenda for the Hong Kong Ministerial meeting of December 2005 were services, agriculture, non-agricultural market access, and special and differential treatment for developing countries. The draft of the Hong Kong declaration agreed on 18 December 2005, mentions further liberalization in Mode 3; that is, the `commercial presence' category of service providers. This is expected to foster increased FDI in a vast gamut of service sectors, such as banking, insurance, construction and engineering, tourism, education, telecommunications, and professional services. It also provides for removal or substantial reduction of economic needs tests in countries, such as relaxing the norm that local employment should be generated. India should utilize the opportunities that liberalization has provided, in attracting FDI in the services sector to the optimum, and regulate it for growth.

References

Arora, A. & Athreye, S. 2001. *The Software Industry and India's Economic Development*. Information Economics and Policy. Pittsburgh: Carnegie Mellon University. Retrieved November 21, 2010 from http://www.heinz.cmu.edu

Desai, A.V. 2000. *The Peril and the Promises: Broader Implications of the Indian Presence in Information Technologies*. Center for Research on Economic Development and Policy Reform. Working Paper No.70. California: Stanford University. Retrieved April 4, 2008 from http://www.stanford.edu

Economic Survey, 2001-2002, 2004-2005, 2006-2007, Reserve Bank of India. Mumbai

Mehta, S. 2004. *The IT Industry in India: Strategic Review*. New Delhi: National Association of Software and Service Companies

Moosa, I. A. 2002. *FDI-Theory, Evidence, and Service Companies*. New York: Palgrave

Patra, M.D. & Kapur, M. 2003. *India's Workers Remittances: A User's Lament about Balance of Payments Compilation*. 16th Meeting of the IMF Committee on Balance of Payments Statistics. Washington D.C. December 1-5

Reserve Bank of India Annual Report. 2001-2, 2004-5, 2006-7

Reserve Bank of India 2002. *Statistics of International Trade in Services*. Report of the Technical group. March

—. 2003. *Financial Performance of FDI Companies in India*. Reserve Bank of India Bulletin. December

Statistical Outline of India 2000-1, 2006-7. Mumbai: Tata Services Limited

Stiglitz, J. 2002. *Globilization and its Discontents.* London: Penguin
United Nations 2002. *Manual of Statistics on International Trade in Services.*
World Development Report 2005, 2006, 2007, 2008
WTO 2003. *Measuring Trade in Services.* World Trade Organization. November. Retrieved July 2, 2010 from http://www.wto.org

CHAPTER THREE

CHARACTERISTICS OF HEALTHY AND UNHEALTHY CHINESE SMALL AND MEDIUM SIZE ENTERPRISES (SMES)

KANITSORN TERDPAOPONG AND YANG YIN

Abstract

In this paper, we will present an empirical study of the financial characteristics in the growing Chinese entrepreneurial SMEs, which were listed in the Chinese Stock Markets during 2006-2009. Of these, 20 percent were State-owned enterprises, and the remaining 80 percent were private. The study examined the structures that are embedded in traditional Chinese culture and values, the ownership structure of Chinese SMEs, and the limitations that they experience regarding expansion and growth. Our findings suggest that healthy Chinese SMEs were financially strong, with the majority of them investing in activities in order to strengthen and promote the growth of the business. The findings indicate a certain uniqueness in the financial characteristics of Chinese SMEs.

Introduction

Over the past two decades, China has achieved great success in economic development. The Chinese National Bureau of Statistics reported that GDP had reached an average of 8 percent in 2008, increasing to 9.2 in 2009, with a further increase in 2010 to reach 10.3 percent year-on-year (Chinadaily 2011). With the start of China's reforms in the late-1970s, SMEs began to flourish, as symbolized by the booming of township and village enterprises (TVEs) in rural areas. After nearly three decades of development, the number of SMEs in China amounts to over 22 million (China Labor Statistical Yearbook 2005); the share of SMEs in the total number of enterprises was 99.3 percent in 2004 (Yu 2007). Also since 2006, China has become the prominent country in attracting both foreign currency reserves and international investment. In spite of these facts the achievement was not reflected in the performance of the security markets in Shanghai and Shenzhen. Within these markets, there has been a sharp fall since 2001, and many businesses, for numerous reasons, have failed.

With the introduction of the first Bankruptcy Law, which came into effect on 11 November 1988, many companies, especially non-listed, declared either un-liquidity or bankruptcy. Many researchers estimated that the underlying causes of these features in the markets was contributed through inadequate market transparency, poor government regulation of the market, a lack of sound and reliable models to support the assessment of a company's financial situation, and identification of potential distress (Altman et al. 2007).

These obstacles have a major influence on all types of enterprises in China, whether they are large or small, or private or state-owned enterprises (SOEs). However, in regard to small and medium sized enterprises (SMEs), the challenges are more difficult to resolve. With the enforcement of regulations to delist enterprises suffering financial difficulties from the Chinese stock market in 2001, there was a dramatic increase of interest from both domestic and international market participants. However, other features, such as the structure of equity (e.g., tradable/non-tradable shares), preference for Chinese investors which favours long-term holdings over several years, as well as differences in historical background, all contribute to the seemingly unique financial characteristics of Chinese enterprises.

Thus, it is imperative that a sound and reliable set of indicators are not only identified, but also established to investigate the survivability of Chinese SMEs that are facing financial difficulties. As it is desirable to discern the potential risks and signs of financial failure in advance, the earlier it is possible for the business managers to take effective steps to improve administration before the financial situation of the enterprise becomes a major crisis, the better. This also enables the associated investors and creditors to identify the importance and effects of the risks and implement their own countermeasures.

This research, therefore, aims to distinguish the characteristics separating financially secure SMEs from the financially distressed. The research starts by determining the definitions for financial security and financially stressed firms, as well as the features that characterize SMEs, which are the focus group of this study. The data has been collected from the main securities market of China, which is at Shenzhen. The selection and application of statistical tools is discussed. The variables used in the paper were carefully selected from several different variables identified in previous research.

In Section 2, the paper reviews the literature; and then develops the research hypotheses in Section 3. The research methods are outlined in Section 4. In Section 5, the empirical results of the study are presented and discussed. Finally, in Section 6, the results of the empirical tests are discussed, and conclusions presented.

Literature Review

There are numerous differences between SMEs and large businesses (Hall 1995; Pratten 1991; Tam et al. 2007). The focus of most published literature regarding SMEs refers to external relations, and issues such as industrial services, sub-contracting, inter-business relationships, licensing, networking, and collaborative research and development, while the focus of literature regarding large firms refers more to internal relations (Ledwith 2000). There are many papers that have considered the establishment of a predictive model for the potential of a business failing financially, and the following sections will explore and discuss issues that have been raised in already published papers regarding the financial situations of SMEs, and more specifically, of Chinese SMEs.

The importance of SME sustainability due to the substantial contribution SMEs make to most economies concern for their sustainability has become a major issue for policy makers and the business community. The success, or failure, of SMEs will inevitably affect other associated businesses. Encouraging and supporting the growth of SMEs also contributes towards the success of both economic and social objectives, such as expanding workers' skills or alleviating poverty in inner cities or declining regions (Schlogl 2004). In general, the significance of SMEs in the employment sector for creating jobs and stimulating economic growth has been recognised (Bàkiewicz 2005; Veskaisri 2007). For example, SMEs comprise a fundamental unit in the Thai economy, constituting over 99 percent of the total number of enterprises in the country (Thai Office of SMEs Promotion 2007). As a result of this recognition and its importance to the nation's economy, the issue of the sustainability of SMEs has become increasingly important in the development of government policies. For instance, the Thai government has implemented policies to enhance their viability, although the problems associated with the failure of SMEs continue. The economic crisis of 1997 promoted the governments in many countries to have greater concern for economic recovery and growth of SMEs (Bàkiewicz 2005; Swierczek & Ha 2003). However, despite the recent emphasis on SMEs, this sector in the economy has received insufficient research attention (Bàkiewicz 2005).

Against this background, many researchers have developed models for predicting the likelihood of SMEs success or failure using several statistical approaches such as multiple discriminant analysis (MDA), logistic regression (LOGIT), probit analysis (PROBIT), and Linear probability model (LPM). All of these models have the objective of identifying financial concerns as a potential early warning of potential financial failure, and therefore, facilitate other decision makers to understand the financial profile of businesses (Ahn et al. 2000), and inform policy-makers by highlighting key priority areas. As SMEs tend to exhibit risk characteristics that are different from those of large corporations, an understanding of these features assists greatly in the development of measures to prevent future failure. It is apparent that there is limited literature on the financial risks for Chinese SMEs in general, and since the importance of SMEs and the tendency in increasing of SMEs (Hutchinson & Michaelas 2000) cannot be overlooked, their financial characteristics deserve attention. This being so, this paper seeks to provide further empirical evidence required for the acknowledgement and identification of financial characteristics of Chinese SMEs.

Difficulties Faced by SMEs

The available literature is rich with anecdotal and empirical data about the inadequate financial resources as a primary cause of SMEs failure (Coleman 2000; Van Auken & Neeley 1996). The reliance on private markets limits the types of financing SMEs can receive. The study by Berger and Udell (1998) stated that financial limitations, coupled with the small firm's initial use of internal sources of capital, resulted in a unique situation in which capital structure decisions are made. Cancer and Knez-Riedl (2005) noted that many companies used the concept of cash flow to support short-term decisions. SMEs seek adequate funding for their business in order to remain viable (Huang et al. 2002). These strategies can include attracting sufficient funds, creating external links with other companies, having skilled employees, taking risks, and using networks; all of which actually add burden to the already financially stressed SMEs for their continued success (Vermeulen 2005). Weinberg (1994) stated that the access of SMEs to information regarding investment is limited, thereby inhibiting their ability for possible investment and potential growth. Spanos et al. (2001) concluded that SMEs face difficulties of size-related disadvantages, limited access to the skills of employees, lack of advanced and high technology skills, and limited access to good quality financial resources, many of which caused SMEs to focus on gaining access to new and high cost resources.

Understandably, SMEs are not financially equipped to compete directly against large firms because of their limited resources (Hyder & Abraha 2004). However, this should not belie the fact that, even with limited resources, the competitive nature of SMEs often allows them to protect their specialized niche markets in which they generate sufficient profits, regardless of the size of their market share (Lambert & Cooper 2000). Several challenges that SMEs confront have been identified, and these obstacles are best summarized in the conclusion of a paper for the Committee for the Promotion of SMEs in Thailand. These challenges fall within the following four categories: (1) Limited financial resources; (2) Loss of competitive advantage in the market place; (3) Lack of good internal administration; and (4) Ineffective support from government (Office of SMEs Promotion 2006, 2007).

In China, SMEs foster market diversification, promote innovation, and provide many employment opportunities. Yet the development of viable and efficient SMEs is hampered by several constraints. Lack of capital is becoming the predominant financial difficulty because SMEs are credit insufficient and vulnerable to credit crunches during financial crises. Compared to medium-sized enterprises, the smaller enterprises, especially those that are privately and individually owned, have to deal with the obstacle of raising the initial investment, let alone on-going finances (Tambunan 2008).

Most small enterprises get their initial capital by the owner/operator personally borrowing from relatives or friends, as commercial banks are not willing to loan to them with their low credit ranking (Yuan & Vinig 2007). Apart from financial difficulty, some other common constraints include difficulties in procuring raw materials, lack of access to relevant business information, difficulties in marketing and distribution, low technological capabilities, high transportation costs, human resource problems, concerns caused by cumbersome and costly bureaucratic procedures, and policies and regulations that generate market distortions, especially corporate operating management challenges. As China only emerged from a fully controlled economy in 1992, it can still be considered as an emerging nation on the world economic stage with most of the state-owned enterprises yet to be privatized. So, effective corporate management systems are still being formulated, introduced and established in most large-sized enterprises, let alone in SMEs (Barth et al. 2011).

Definition of SMEs
The available literature shows that SMEs are identified in various ways in different countries, based on several characteristics such as the amount

of total and fixed assets, total sales volume, the number of employees, or by a combination of these factors. For instance, within the manufacturing business sector of Australia, small enterprises are those that employ <100 people and medium enterprises are those that employ >100, but <200 people (Holmes & Kent 1991; Meredith 1982). In the US, the classification of businesses is also based on the number of employees. They are classified as very small enterprises if they employ <20 people, as small enterprises if they employ between 20 and 100 people, and as medium enterprises if they employ between 100 and 500 (Office of Advocacy 1984).

Altman and Sabato (2007), by adapting the definition of SMEs of the new Basel Accord, considered SMEs to be businesses with sales volume <US$65m. The European Commission, whose definition is used by many countries, states that SMEs are companies that employ <250 staff and have an annual turnover not exceeding EUR 50m, or an annual balance sheet total not exceeding EUR 43m (European Commission 2003). China, Indonesia, Japan, Korea, Malaysia, and Singapore also use the number of employees as the basis for classifying firms, with different levels used as cut-off points (Khader & Gupta 2002). In China, SMEs include state-owned SMEs, urban concentration SMEs, township enterprises, and private and individual enterprises. Most SMEs are non-state-owned. SMEs in China are involved in many major economic sectors: industry (including manufacturing, mining, electricity, production and supply of fuel gas and domestic water), construction, transportation, the postal service, wholesale and retail sales, lodging and catering. These are classified as SMEs in terms of sales and/or the amount of total assets, as well as the number of employees. The classification criteria is summarised in Table 1.

Forms and Consequences of Business Failure

Business failure can take several forms, including excessive liability, financial deficit, insolvency, default, distress, non-performing loans, business termination, and/or bankruptcy and liquidation (Kraus & Litzenberger 1973). Interestingly, some firms experiencing financial difficulties manage to survive in the market place without ceasing to operate or declaring bankruptcy. Bernanke et al. (1988) argue that bankruptcy costs are actually quite small, and can often be avoided by the renegotiation of debt terms or by the acquisition of the firm by a third party. However, the most important costs occur when firms are close to bankruptcy, for this is when access to loans from financial institutions or further investment from interested parties, as well as obtaining credit from suppliers, who are hesitant to enter long-term financial agreements to take advantage of productive or market opportunities.

These difficulties reduce SMEs' ability to gain finance on reasonable terms, and thus the ability to continue to operate profitably within the market, which results in the firms moving closer to declaring bankruptcy. To determine the actual cost of business failure is often difficult because the line between business success and failure is not always clear. Branch (2002) categorized bankruptcy-related costs into four different areas: (1) Real costs borne by the distressed firms; (2) Real costs directly borne by the claimants; (3) Losses to the distressed firms that are offset by gains to other firms; and, (4) Real costs borne by parties other than the distressed firms and/or its claimants. Branch's (2002) study showed that the claimants recovered approximately 56 percent of the bankrupt firms' pre-distress value (PDV). Dealing with financial distress, total bankruptcy-related costs to firms and claimants were 13-20 percent of the distressed firms' PDV. Further, indirect bankruptcy costs include the loss of sales, profits, and goodwill. These losses are incurred on account of reduced consumer confidence that results from the individual customer/client's decisions towards the distressed firms and their inability to obtain goods, credit or to issue securities.

Table 1: Size Classification of Chinese SMEs

Sector	Employment(People)	Sales (Million RMB)	Total assets (Million RMB)	Description
Industry	300-2,000	30-300	40-400	The medium enterprise has to reach minimum of the three indices; otherwise, small one.
Construction	600-3,000	30-300	40-400	
Wholesale	100-200	30-300	no require-ments	The medium enterprise has to reach minimum of the two indices; otherwise, small one.
Retail	100-500	10-150		
Transportation	500-3,000	30-300		
Postal service	400-1,000	30-300		
Lodging and catering	400-800	30-150		

Source: Adapted from Temporary Regulations of Standards for SMEs in China (State Economic and Trade Commission 2003)

Beyond these losses, the distressed companies are possibly occupied in taking steps to avoid bankruptcy to the extent that normal business operations are disregarded (Ross et al. 2008; Warner 1977). Therefore, as going bankrupt is expensive, firms will spend resources to avoid it. In addition to the substantial direct and indirect costs of business failure, there are other dimensions to SME failure that should be considered. Firstly, the probability of both personal and business bankruptcy, including the subsequent liquidation is much higher with small enterprises. Secondly, the direct costs of bankruptcy and liquidation fall more heavily in relative terms on small enterprises. Thirdly, there may be some other indirect costs associated with bankruptcy and liquidation that are not readily apparent (Holmes et al. 2003).

Financial Characteristics

A firm's aggregate level of debt tends to be a good starting point for assessing its economic stability. In particular, high levels of debt tend to create real costs at both micro- and macro-economic levels (Bernanke et al. 1988), with both direct and indirect consequences. Nonetheless, the question of 'how high is high?' has always been unanswerable. Firms with high levels of debt are less likely to be able to get favorable terms and conditions for their businesses, and may become bankrupt. The consequences are enormous both to the businesses themselves, and the macro-economy at large.

Unsurprisingly, the possibility of serious consequences of high levels of firm debt seems to engender a high level of attention, yet it has not always been easy to determine the proportion of debt and equity that would maximize the chances of a business to survive economic downturns (Warner 1977). This issue is an important one as failure of SMEs costs society in a variety of ways. Davidson and Dutia (1991) found that small firms have less liquidity and more leveraged than large firms, yet tend to have lower profit margins. In the case of financially distressed firms, the financial characteristics are even more extreme with low liquidity, high leverage and low or negative profits (losses). As financially distressed firms tend to exhibit low liquidity and high levels of long term debt, financial ratios can be examined to predict the chances of business failure.

Variables Used in Previous Research

Several researchers have also used financial characteristics of firms to develop a failure prediction model for both large and small firms. Previous studies, (for example, Altman 1968, 1983, 1993; Beaver 1966; Deakin 1972, 1977; Edmister 1972; McGurr & Devaney 1998) have attempted to formulate sound predictive models to distinguish distressed firms from the non-distressed firms. A study for the prediction of financial distress enterprises in China began in 1999 (Chang-e 2006). Several kinds of research methods have been adopted; for instance, Jing (1999) used Univariate Discriminant Analysis, Ling (2000) adopted the Multiple Discriminant Analysis Model based on the Z-Score developed by Altman and developed the Z-China Score to support the identification of potential distressed firms, while Shu-e and Li (2005) used the Artificial Neural Network Approach. Of these, only a few were associated with SMEs, and this may have occurred because insufficient information of SMEs was available.

Nonetheless, the study of the variables used in previous studies can benefit the undertaking of research and investigation of Chinese SMEs. Most researchers constructed failure prediction models using the variables such as CA/TL (current assets to total liability ratio), CA/TA (current asset to total assets ratio), CL/TA (current liability to total assets ratio), debt/equity ratio, WC/TA (working capital to total assets ratio), WC/TL (working capital to total liability ratio), cash flow/current liabilities, LL/TA (long-term liability to total assets ratio), TL/TA (total liability to total assets ratio), sales/total assets ratio, EBIT/Sales (earnings before interest and tax expenses to total sales), EBIT/TA (earnings before interest and tax expenses to total assets), EAIT/TA (earnings after interest and tax expenses to total assets), and market value equity/total liabilities.

Methodology

The research focuses on SMEs as listed on the China SMEs Listed Boards in Shenzhen. A total of 359 companies were selected, utilizing the secondary data available on-line resources, such as publically available financial statements. A total of 957 financial statements of the selected China SMEs were collected from 2006-2009 (4 years), and were used to determine the differences between financially stressed and non-financially stressed SMEs as represented on the Shenzhen Stock Exchange.

This study employed parametric (Independent and Dependent Paired Sample T-Test) and non-parametric (Mann-Whitney U Test) approaches in the Statistical Package for the Social Sciences (SPSS) program in the process of data analysis. The validity of the study was limited to the reliability of the financial ratios collected from on-line financial statements of the listed SMEs. The study employed an analysis of many financial ratios that were able to differentiate financially stressed firms from non-financially stressed firms, using three significance levels 0.05, 0.01 and 0.001.

There are several terms that need to be defined clearly, and in the correct context so that these key terms are understood and applied correctly to the results within the scope of this research paper by fellow scholars, economists and other interested parties.

Table 2: Variable Definition

LIQUIDITY MEASURES			
1	CACL	CURRENT ASSETS TO CURRENT LIABILIITY RATIO (UNIT: TIME)	Cash, account receivables, bills, inventory, other current assets divided by current liability
2	WCTA	WORKING CAPITAL TO TOTAL ASSETS RATIO (UNIT : PER CENT)	Current assets less current liability as a percent of total assets
3	CFCL	CASH FLOW TO CURRENT LIABILITY RATIO (UNIT: PER CENT)	Net total cash flow as a percent of current liability
LEVERAGE MEASURES			
4	LLTA	LONG TERM LIABILITY TO TOTAL ASSETS RATIO (UNIT: PER CENT)	Long-term liabilities as a percent of total assets
5	TLTA	TOTAL LIABILITY TO TOTAL ASSETS RATIO (UNIT: PER CENT)	Short-term and long-term liabilities as a percent of total assets
6	DE	DEBT TO EQUITY RATIO (UNIT: TIME)	Debt divided by equity
PROFITABILITY MEASURES			
7	TITA	TOTAL INCOME TO TOTAL ASSETS RATIO (UNIT: PER CENT)	Total core and other income as a percent of total assets
8	INTEBIT	INTEREST TO EARNINGS (UNIT: PER CENT)	Interest expenses as a percent of earnings before interest and tax expenses
9	EBITTA	EARNINGS BEFORE INTEREST AND TAX EXPENSES TO TOTAL ASSETS RATIO (UNIT: PER CENT)	All earnings before interest and tax expenses as a percent of total assets
10	EAITTA	EARNINGS AFTER INTEREST AND TAX EXPENSES TO TOTAL ASSETS RATIO (UNIT: PER CENT)	All earnings after interest and tax expenses as a percent of total assets

As outlined in the preceding section, the commonly used features for categorizing the size of firms include the number of employees, the amount of fixed assets, the volume of sales, the balance sheet outstanding, and the structure of shareholders. Even though the number of employees is the most frequently used criterion in most countries around the world, this information was not available regarding enterprises in China, since there is no information centre where this data can be collected. Therefore, in this study the firms that were listed on the SME board of the Shenzhen Stock Exchange are used as being representative of Chinese SMEs.

A 'non-financially distressed' or 'healthy' SME refers to a firm that has no distressed qualities illustrated through the following criteria: bond default, bank loan default, delisting of a company, government intervention via special financing, the filing for bankruptcy and liquidation. In this study, the 'healthy' qualities of a firm also include the presence of a positive operating cash flow and profit at the time the sample was taken. The 769 financial statements (e.g., balance sheets, comprehensive income, and statements of cash flow) of the companies listed on the Shenzhen Stock Exchange between 2006 and 2009 that showed healthy qualities were used as samples of non-financially distressed SMEs.

The companies that were listed on the Shenzhen Stock Exchange between 2006-2009 which had 'unhealthy' or 'financially distressed' qualities, such as those firms that had defaulted on bonds and loans, had sought financial aid through government intervention and showed negative operating cash flow and low profit margins were used to represent the unhealthy or financially stressed firms. Of the SMEs that possessed these qualities on the Chinese Stock Markets, a total 188 financial statements were collected and used in the present study.

With these two different groups of SMEs: healthy (769), and unhealthy (188) samples; making a total of 957 sets of financial statements, a total of 10 independent variables were selected based on: (1) The most commonly used in previous studies; and, (2) The availability of the data. As defined in Table 2, these variables were divided into three categories: (1) Liquidity refers to how quickly and cheaply an asset can be converted into cash or in other words the ability of current assets to meet current liabilities when due; (2) Leverage, also known as gearing or levering, refers to the use of debt to supplement investment or the degree to which a business is utilizing borrowed money; and, (3) Profitability refers to an ability of a firm to generate net income on a consistent basis.

Hypotheses

To understand the usefulness of the results obtained from the investigation of financial ratios it is necessary to examine the differences presented in these features by both non-financially and financially stressed enterprises. Thus, by categorizing the ratios into liquidity, leverage and profitability ratios, the following hypothesis and the related sub-hypotheses can be applied to the SMEs in China.

Hypothesis One: (H_1):   There are significant differences in the financial ratios of non-financially distressed and financially distressed Chinese SMEs.

$H_{1.1}$:   The liquidity of the non-financially distressed Chinese SMEs is higher than that of financially distressed Chinese SMEs. Variables used in clarifying the term 'LIQUIDITY' include:
   $H_{1.1.1}$ CACL: Current assets to current liability ratio
   $H_{1.1.2}$ WCTA: Working capital to total assets ratio
   $H_{1.1.3}$ CFCL: Cash flow to current liability ratio

$H_{1.2}$:   The financial leverage of the non-financially distressed Chinese SMEs is less than that of financially distressed Chinese SMEs. Variables used in clarifying the term 'financial leverage' include:
   $H_{1.2.1}$ LLTA: Long-term liability to total assets ratio
   $H_{1.2.2}$ TLTA: Total liability to total assets ratio
   $H_{1.2.3}$ DE: Debt to equity ratio

$H_{1.3}$:   The profitability of the non-financially distressed Chinese SMEs is higher than that of financially distressed Chinese SMEs. Variables used in clarifying the term 'profitability' include:
   $H_{1.3.1}$ TITA: Total income to total assets ratio
   $H_{1.3.2}$ INTEBIT: Interest expense to earnings before interest and tax ratio
   $H_{1.3.3}$ EBITTA: Earnings before interest and tax expenses to total assets ratio
   $H_{1.3.4}$ EAITTA: Earnings after interest and tax expenses to total assets ratio

Results and Discussion

The sample of the study was the 359 firms that were listed on the China SMEs Listed Board in Shenzhen. The total number of companies listed on the SME board to date (3 March 2011) was 564 in total. Therefore, the sample of the study comprises about 64 percent of total SMEs listed board in Shenzhen. Table 3 demonstrates that there is a majority of 78 percent (283 companies) that are private enterprises, with the remaining 21 percent (76 companies) being state-owned enterprises (SOEs). Of these 55 percent had been established for 6-10 years, with the longest established company being a private enterprise that was established in 1905, Zhejiang Kan Specialities Material Co., Ltd (Table 4).

To illustrate the financial status of the enterprises chosen for this study (Table 5), we investigated the means of several important business ratios. For instance, asset size on average of the non-distressed SMEs was about 1,300 million RMB (US$84m) while for distressed SMEs this was 1,582 million RMB (US$227m). The equity mean for the non-distressed SMEs is 713 million RMB (US$101m), which is quite similar to that of distressed SMEs.

Table 3: Listed SMEs Establishing Status Classification

Type	Total Listed SMEs (company)	Listed SMEs (%)
State Own Enterprises (SOEs)	76	21.17
Private Enterprises	283	78.83
Total	359	100.00

Source: Adapted from Shenzhen Stock Exchange (http://szse.cn/main/en/)

Table 4: Listed SMES Year of Establishment Classification

Years Est	Total Listed SMEs	Total Listed SMEs (%)	Establishing status (company)		Establish status (%)	
			SOEs	Private		
1–5 yrs	26	7.24	4	22	1.11	6.13
6–10 yrs	196	54.60	49	147	13.65	40.95
11–20 yrs	128	35.65	21	107	5.85	29.81
21–30 yrs	8	2.23	2	6	0.56	1.67
> 30 years	1	0.28	0	1	0.00	0.28
Total	359	100.00	76	283	21.17	78.83

Source: Adapted from Shenzhen Stock Exchange (http://szse.cn/main/en/)

The study also examined the differences between non-financially stressed and financially distressed SMEs in China by using a parametric (Independent sample T-Test) and a non-parametric (Mann-Whitney U Test) to test the set hypothesis.

Liquidlity

Non-financially distressed firms had liquidity significantly higher when compared to that of distressed firms when taking into account the resulting calculated ratio means of CACL (current assets to current liability) and CFCL (cash flow to current liability). The results on parametric *t*-test showed statistical significance on CACL ratio; t (955) = 5.862, p>.05 and Z = -3.629 and on CFCL ratio; t (955) = 4.674, p>.05 and Z = -3.889.

It is of significance that non-distressed firms possessed higher current assets when compared to that of distressed firms, with the net cash flow being over 60 percent of current liabilities. Yet, only these two variables showed the different financial characteristic between the two groups with both the parametric and non-parametric tests. From this result, we accept the hypotheses 1.1.1 and 1.1.3, and due to the non-significance on the non-parametric Mann-Whitney U Test on WCTA ratio we then disprove the hypothesis 1.1.2.

Leverage

The long-term liability to total assets ratio did not show a significant difference between the two groups where parametric *t*-test and non-parametric Mann-Whitney U Test provided the same result of the non-significance (t (955) = -.776, p>.05 and Z -.19). This may be because of the main use of the short-term liability rather than of long-term one. The ratio of current liability to total liability of the healthy firms amounted to 32.82 per cent, however total liability, which included both current and long-term liability, to total assets ratio, amounted to 37.38 per cent and these ratios were similar when compared to that of stressed firms, with the results of 42.51 per cent on CLTA and 47.59 per cent on TLTA. Enterprises in both groups possessed a high equity proportion; with non-financially stressed firms having a result greater than 60 percent; and in the case of financially distressed enterprises at 50 percent. Furthermore, the mean result of the debt to equity ratio on the parametric test did not present the significant difference between the two groups. We then accept the hypothesis 1.2.2; but disprove 1.2.1 and 1.2.3.PROFITABILITYThe results did not illustrate significant differences of the INTEBIT ratio where the standard deviation of the ratio was very high, nor did the TITA ratio.

Both parametric and non-parametric tests provided the same results of non-significance of TITA: t (955) = 0.67, p>.05, Z = -.383 and of INTEBIT; t (955) = .82, p>.05, Z = -.134.

Table 5: Means of Important Items of Chinese SME: Averages of 4 Years 2006-2009

Items	Non-Distressed SMEs		Distressed SMEs	
	Means (RMB M.)	Means (USD M.)*	Means (RMB M.)	Means (USD M.)*
Current assets	771.72	108.92	1,119.45	160.50
Total assets	1,299.92	183.59	1,581.87	226.47
Current liabilities	499.03	70.28	761.64	109.07
Long-term liabilities	484.39	82.44	886.64	126.97
Equity	712.83	100.77	693.96	99.30
Earnings before interest and tax expenses	143.18	20.13	74.69	10.57
Earnings after interest and tax expenses	91.25	12.92	42.89	6.06

*Items of year 2006 converted to USD using exchange rate 1 Yuan = 0.128138 USD (29 Dec 2006);
Items of year 2007 converted to USD using exchange rate 1 Yuan = 0.137088 USD (31 Dec 2007);
Items of year 2008 converted to USD using exchange rate 1 Yuan = 0.146574 USD (31 Dec 2008); Items of year 2009 converted to USD using exchange rate 1 Yuan = 0.146477 USD (31 Dec 2009);
Data source: Financial information, http://www.szse.cn/main/en/ (Shenzhen Stock Exchange, 2010);
Data source: Exchange rate source, http://www.x-rates.com/cgi-bin/hlookup.cgi (X-Rates, 2011)

However, the profitability differences can still be observed through the EBITTA and EAITTA ratios, which showed the significance of both the parametric and non-parametric approaches - EBITTA: t (955) = 4.082, p>.05, Z= -8.433 and EAITTA: t (955) = 8.577, p>.05, Z = -9.133. Thus the hypotheses 1.3.3 and 1.3.4 were then accepted. Even though not every variable showed significant differences between the two groups, the results still lead us to the sound conclusion that liquidity and profitability of the non-financially distressed enterprises, or the "healthy" SMEs; were greater when compared to the financially stressed enterprises or the "unhealthy" SMEs. The healthy firms had greater liquidity than the unhealthy firms by showing greater current assets than current liability, which supports the conclusion that healthy firms held greater cash flow than their current obligations. With the result of non-significance of TITA and INTTA ratios, we consider that both healthy and non-healthy firms had similar ratios of total income and interest expense when compared with total assets. This is also aligned with the LLTA and DE ratios in which no statistical significances were found. This brings us to the conclusion that the funding resource of both groups came from the combination of their own funding (equity) of over 50 per cent, with other funds being raised through short-term liability, which was mainly sourced from creditors, suppliers, and loans from banking institutions. However short-term liability seems to be a financial concern for both groups, even though these firms were listed on the stock exchange, to raise funds for capital investment on the open market, or direct financing presents a challenge. While both healthy and non-healthy firms seem to obtain few loans through banking institutions, this may be because of the high associated fees and costs of bank loans to SMEs. It is harder to evaluate the difficulties that confront the unlisted SMEs.

The results also support the conclusion that the unhealthy firms faced difficulties in several areas of business, such as the cost of manufacturing goods, distribution costs, and the final cost to the consumer, as well as the internal administrative and general expenses (the significant difference of EBITTA ratio) with both groups having to confront high taxation costs due to the significance of the EAITTA ratio; especially during the international economic crisis when the costs of export trading were higher than usual. When taxation costs and fees account for 20 percent of the total business costs (Zhou et al. 2010), including tax incentives for SMEs, the simple solution would appear to be the lowering of tax rates and increased tax relief, yet this requires the support of the relevant organizations such as government departments and commercial banking institutions.

Characteristics of Healthy and Unhealthy Chinese SMEs

Table 6: T-Test and Mann Whitney U-Test Summary

H	Mean		Std. Deviation		T-Test		Mann Whitney U-Test	
	HEALTHY	UNHEALTHY	HEALTHY	UNHEALTHY	Sig	t	Sig	Z
Liquidity								
H1.1.1	3.03	1.93	4.44	1.48	.000***	5.682	.000***	-3.629
H1.1.2	28.54	23.28	24.95	27.43	.011*	2.539	.098 NS	-1.657
H1.1.3	66.94	12.59	289.97	69.77	.000***	4.674	.000***	-3.889
Financial								
H1.2.1	4.56	5.08	7.78	9.88	.438 NS	-0.776	.849 NS	-.190
H1.2.2	37.38	47.59	21.20	18.04	.000***	-6.025	.000***	-6.835
H1.2.3	.77	2.13	.77	14.91	.215NS	-1.244	.000***	-6.530
Profitability								
H1.3.1	82.14	78.12	78.53	48.80	.503 NS	0.670	.702 NS	-0.383
H1.3.2	13.32	-8.17	21.85	359.24	.413 NS	0.820	.893 NS	-0.134
H1.3.3	10.44	4.87	17.97	10.46	.000***	4.082	.000***	-8.433
H1.3.4	7.52	2.27	5.49	7.93	.000***	8.577	.000***	-9.133

***Significance at .1% level (0.001)

** Significance at 1% level (0.01)*   Significant at 5% level   (0.05)NS: Not significance

Considering the internal financial structure of enterprises within both groups, it was found that the non-financially distressed firms, or the healthy firms, had higher liquidity and profitability than that of the distressed firms, while the distressed firms had higher liability, especially current liability, than that of non-distressed firms. Therefore, the significant statistical findings fail to support the main hypothesis, that only half of the hypothesized ratios were accepted, with the rest disproved.

Conclusions

In this study, we have attempted to identify the differences in the financial characteristics between the non-financially stressed SMEs, or the 'healthy' firms, and those of financially stressed SMEs, or 'unhealthy' firms, in China. The study obtained a total of 957 sets of financial statements for 359 SMEs between 2006 and 2009, with 20 percent being state-owned enterprises, with 80 percent being private enterprises. The differences of the financial characteristics between the two groups were tested and confirmed, and the results of this study were unexpected for the non-financially stressed companies, understandably, exhibited a better financial performance when compared to the financially distressed companies, yet this was not supported in every ratio we tested. The characteristics of the non-distressed companies included high liquidity and profitability, with low debt, while stressed companies were characterized with low liquidity and profitability, but with the burden of carrying high debt. It is important to note that long-term liability to assets ratio of both non-financially distressed and financially distressed firms did not show significant differences, which means both groups did not greatly finance their business with long-term liability but rather on short-term liabilities and equity.

This result contradicts the result of previous researchers, such as of Davidson and Dutia (1991) who found distressed firms had high proportion of long-term liability. This might be as a result of the nature of Chinese enterprises that have a higher tendency to self-invest in their business. Both 'healthy' and 'unhealthy' enterprises tended to obtain short-term, rather than long-term liability. Yet, the current liability and equity facilitated financially stressed SMEs to continue business operations with a degree of profitability. In other countries distressed firms would normally possess a high proportion of both long-term liability to total assets ratio (for example, the ratio may be over 100 percent of total assets such as in the case of Thai distressed SMEs) and total liability to total assets ratio (over 300 percent of total assets in the case of Thai distressed

SMEs; Terdpaopong 2009). However, this is not the case in China. The results enable us to observe the distinguishing financial characteristics and differences between healthy and unhealthy SMEs in China in terms of the percentage of long-term ability to total asset, thus making obvious the unique financial characteristics of the Chinese.

The results of this study have implications in both the fields of financial/economic theory and in practice, and can benefit entrepreneurs and others interested associated parities. The findings can perhaps provide a satisfactory framework for meaningful analysis in the future. The continued sustainability of SMEs underpins the stability and strength of worldwide economies. There is a need to develop a systematic study of the precursor signs of potential business failure, thus extending and expanding upon the already existing body of knowledge and hopefully reduce the number of SMEs that fail and/or declare bankruptcy. There are a number of areas that require further academic focus, such as the establishment of a clear and concise definition of financially distressed SMEs used in academic research, including the identification of the causes of failure and other difficulties faced by SMEs, the identification of the indicators of potential future failure and the development of sophisticated mathematical models for predicting potential failures. The model for predicting the possibility of future failure should be in place in order to provide a warning and thereby assist stakeholders and other interested parties when they have to consider the allocation of resources of financially stressed SMEs. Of course, this requires both the Chinese government and private agencies to establish a reliable industry database and develop a successful model in order to provide some facilities for SMEs development with a means of predicting the potential future financial collapse of an enterprise. In the emerging economy of China, where the free market has not yet completely taken hold, a company's failure is possibly harder to predict and, to some extent, even harder to characterise due to the degree of protection provided by the government.

References

Ahn, B.S., Cho, S.S. & Kim, C.Y. 2000. The integrated methodology of rough set theory and artificial neural network for business failure prediction. *Expert Systems with Applications.* 18:65-74

Altman, E.I. 1968. Financial ratios, discriminant analysis and the prediction of corporate bankruptcy. *Journal of Finance.* 23(4):589-609

—. 1983. *Corporate Financial Distress: A Complete Guide to Predicting, Avoiding, and Dealing with Bankruptcy.* New York: John Wiley

—. 1993. *Corporate financial distress and bankruptcy: A complete guide to predicting and avoiding distress and profiting from bankruptcy.* New York: John Wiley

Altman, E.I., Heine, M.L., Zhang, L. & Yen, J. 2007. *Corporate Financial Distress Diagnosis in China.* New York: New York University

Altman, E.I. & Sabato, G. 2007. Modelling Credit Risk for SMEs: Evidence from the U.S.Market. *Abacus Journal.* 43(3):332-357

Bàkiewicz, A. 2005. Small and medium Enterprises in Thailand: Following the Leader. *Asia and Pacific Studies.* 2(1)

Barth, J.R., Lin, D. & Yost, K. 2011. Small and Medium Enterprise Financing in Transition Economies. *Atlantic Economic Journal.* 39(1):19-38

Beaver, W.H. 1966. Financial ratios as predictors of failure. *Journal of Accounting Research.* 4:71-111

Berger, A.N. & Udell, G.F. 1998. The economics of small business finance: The roles of private equity and debt markets in the financial growth cycle. *Journal of Banking & Finance.* 22:613-674

Bernanke, B.S., Campbell, J. Y. & Friedman, B.M. 1988. Is There a Corporate Debt Crisis? *Brookings Institution Press.*1:83-139

Branch, B. 2002. The Costs of Bankruptcy: A Review. *International Review of Financial Analysis.* 11(1):39-57

Cancer, V. & Knez-Riedl, J. 2005. Why and how to evaluate the creditworthiness of SMEs' business partners (Small and medium-sized businesses). *International Small Business Journal.* 23(21):143

Chang-e, S. 2006. The Causes and Salvation Ways of Financial Distress Companies-An Empirical Research on the Listed Companies in China. *Journal of Modern Accounting and Auditing.* 2(10):1-9

Chinadaily 2011. China Economy by Numbers. *China Daily.* Retrieved January 21, 2011 from http://www.chinadaily.com.cn

China Labor Statistical Yearbook 2005. Beijing, China: China Statistics Press

Coleman, S. 2000. Access to capital and terms of credit: A comparison of men and women-owned small business. *Journal of Small Business Management,* 38(4):37-53

Davidson, W.N. & Dutia, D. 1991. Debt, liquidity and profitability problems in small firms. *Entrepreneurship: Theory and Practice.* 16(1):53-64

Deakin, E.B. 1972. A discriminant analysis of predictors of business failure. *Journal of Accounting Research.* 10(2):167-179

—. (Ed.). 1977. *Business Failure Prediction: An Empirical Analysis.* New York: Wiley

Edmister, R.O. 1972. An empirical test of financial ratio analysis for small business failure prediction. *Journal of Financial and Quantitative Analysis.* 7(March):1477-1493

European Commission 2003. Commission recommendation: Definition of small & medium sized enterprises. *Official Journal of the European Union.* 1422:39. Retrieved June 13, 2009 from http:www.eif.org

Hall, G. C. 1995. *Surviving and prospering in the small firm sector.* New York: Rutledge.

Holmes, S., Hutchinson, P., Forsaith, D., Gibson, B. & McMahon, R. 2003. *Small Enterprise Finance*: Melbourne: John Wiley

Holmes, S. & Kent, P. 1991. An Empirical Analysis of the Financial Structure of Small and Large Australian Manufacturing Enterprises. *Journal of Small Business Management.* 1(2):141-154

Huang, X., Soutar, G.N. & Brown, A. 2002. New product development process in small and medium-sized enterprises: Some Australian evidence. *Journal of Small Business Management.* 40(1):27-42

Hutchinson, P. & Michaelas, N. (Eds.). 2000. *The Current State of Business Disciplines* (Vol. 3). Rohtak, India: Spellbound Publications

Hyder, A.S. & Abraha, D. 2004. Product and skills development in small and medium-sized high-tech firms through international strategic alliances. *Singapore Management Review.* 26(24):1

Jing, C. 1999. The Empirical Analysis of Financial Worsening Prediction of Listed Company. *Accounting Research.* 4:31-38

Khader, S.A. & Gupta, C.P. (Eds.). 2002. *Enhancing SME Competitiveness in the Age of Globalization.* Tokyo: National Statistical Coordination Board, Asian Productivity Organization.

Kraus, A. & Litzenberger, R.H. 1973. A State-Preference Model of Optimal Financial Leverage. *Journal of Finance.* 28(4):911-922

Lambert, D. & Cooper, M. 2000. Issues in supply chain management. *Industrial Marketing Management.* 29(1):65-83

Ledwith, A. 2000. Management of new product development in small electronics firms. *Journal of European Industrial Training.* 24(2/3/4):137

McGurr, P.T. & Devaney, S.A. 1998. A retail failure prediction model. *International Review of Retail, Distribution and Consumer Research.* 8(3):259-279

Meredith, G.G. 1982. *Small Business Management in Australia.* 2nd ed. Sydney: McGraw-Hill

Office of Advocacy 1984. *The State of Small Business: A Report of the President.* Washington D.C.: Small Business Administration

Office of SMEs Promotion 2006. *White Paper, in Export and Import by SMEs*.
—. 2007. *White Paper, in Export and Import by SMEs*.
Pratten, C. 1991. *The Competitivenss of Small Firms*. Cambridge: Cambridge University Press
Ross, S.A., Westerfield, R.W. & Jordan, B.D. 2008. *Corporate Finance Fundamentals*. New York: McGraw-Hill Irwin
Schlogl, H. 2004. Small and medium enterprises: Seizing the potential. *OECD Observer*. 1(3):46
Shu-e, Y. & Li, H. 2005. Financial Prediction Model of Listed Company under BP Neural Network. *System Engineering Theory and Practice Journal*. 1:12-18
Spanos, Y., Prastakos, G. & Papadakos, V. 2001. Greek firms and EU: Contrasting SMEs and large-sized enterprises. *European Management Journal*. 19(6):638-648
Shenzhen Stock Exchange 2010. *SME Board Data*. Retrieved September 15, 2010 from http://www.szse.cn/main/en/
State Economic and Trade Commision 2003. *The State Development Planning Commission*
Swierczek, F.W. & Ha, T.T. 2003. Entrepreneurial orientation, uncertainty avoidance and firm performance: An analysis of Thai and Vietnamese SMEs. *International Journal of Entrepreneurship and Innovation*. 4(1):46-58
Tam, F.Y., Moon, K.L., Ng, S.F. & Hui, C.L. 2007. Production sourcing strategies and buyer-supplier relationship: A study of the differences between small and large enterprises in Hong Kong colthing industry. *Journal of Fashion Marketing and Management*. 11(2):297-306
Tambunan, T. 2008. SME development, economic growth, and government intervention in a developing country: The Indonesian story. *Journal of International Entrepreneureship*. 6(4):147-167
Terdpaopong, K. 2009. *How financially distressed SMEs could be distinguished from the successful ones in Thailand's market*. Paper presented at the AGSE, Adelaide, Australia, 3-6 February
Van Auken, H.E. & Neeley, L. 1996. Evidence of bootstrap financing among small start-up firms. *Journal of Entrepreneurial and Small Business Finance*. 5(3):235-249
Vermeulen, P.A. 2005. Uncovering barriers to complex incremental product innovation in small and medium-sized financial services firms. *Journal of Small Business Management*. 43(21):432

Veskaisri, K. 2007. The Relationship Between Stragic Planning and Growth in Small and Medium Enterprises (SMEs) in Thailand. *RU International Journal.* 1(1):55-67

Warner, J.B. 1977. Bankruptcy costs: Some evidence. *Journal of Finance.* 2:337-347

Weinberg, J.A. 1994. Firm size, finance, and investment. *Economics Quarterly.* 80(1):19

Yu, J. 2007. *SME Development and Poverty Reduction: Case study of Xiji County, China.* Retrieved January 15, 2011, from http://cfed.org

Yuan, N. & Vinig, T. 2007. Ownership Structure of Chinese SME's and the Challenges it Presents to Their Growth. *Sprouts:Working Papers on Information Systems.* 7(2):1-21

Zhou, J., Guo, T. & Lu, S. 2010. SME law and policy analysis. *Journal of US-China Public Administration.* 7(5):79-82

CHAPTER FOUR

AN ENTREPRENEURIAL INTERNATIONAL JOINT VENTURE: A CASE STUDY INTERFACING THE USA, THAILAND AND INDIA

PAUL HUGHES

Abstract

The international entrepreneur is a relative 'newcomer' and neophyte to international business research. This paper presents an international new venture (INV) case study of an American international entrepreneurial (IE) firm and its business startup and creation issues in Thailand. By using qualitative analysis techniques and in-depth interviews with the company owners, a detailed view of the INV processes involved and the decisions required by these international entrepreneurs for employing semi-skilled Thai operators and highly-skilled analysts from India are presented. An eclectic concepts approach is used to explain the INV business dynamics, interactions, and implications.

Introduction

The concept of the entrepreneur and the corresponding field of entrepreneurship have enjoyed significant study and analysis; entrepreneurships are vitally important to the economic development of a nation (Lado & Vozikis 1996). From the early part of the 20th century, business researchers have attempted to clearly define its persona. Knight (1921) linked entrepreneurship with risk taking; Cole (1968) associated the concepts of both creation and maintenance of profit-oriented ventures to the entrepreneur. Stevenson, Robert, and Grousbeck (1985) defined the entrepreneur as one who can perceive opportunities and act upon them, while Gartner (1985), Rumelt (1987), and Vesper (1990), among others, defined entrepreneurship as the area of new ventures creation (Lado & Vozikis 1996).

Literature Review

The international entrepreneur (IE), as compared to the domestic counterpart, has a much more recent origin of birth. Researchers Zahra and George (2002) indicate that the term 'international entrepreneurship' first appeared in a short article by Morrow (1988). Soon thereafter, McDougall (1989) delivered an empirical study which compared new domestic ventures with entrepreneurial business startups that were geared solely towards a new international venture in another country.

Started by individuals or small groups of entrepreneurs, international new ventures (INVs) are said to own certain valuable assets, to use alliances and network structures to control a relatively large percentage of vital assets, and to have a unique resource that provides a sustainable advantage that is transferable to a foreign location (McDougall et al.1994; Oviatt & McDougall 1994; Oviatt & McDougall 2005).

Thus, in a short span of time, the academic study and theoretical research in this newly coined area of international entrepreneurship analysis was well on its way (Oviatt & McDougall 2005). International business scholars Wright and Ricks (1994) highlighted international entrepreneurship as a newly emerging research arena, and it became clear that arena included: (1) Comparisons of entrepreneurial behaviour in multiple countries and cultures, as well as (2) Organization behaviour that extends across national borders and is entrepreneurial in nature (Oviatt & McDougall 2005).

Knight and Cavusgil (2004) indicate that what was often being seen in new international venture development were companies designed initially, from an early stage, to operate their business on a global scale. Termed as 'born-global' firms, these companies were emerging in increasing and substantial numbers worldwide. They also state that, despite having limited and scarce financial, human, and tangible resources, the international entrepreneurs would leverage innovation, specific knowledge, and any capability within their reach to achieve and sustain international market success. It seems the flexibility possessed by these young, small, and agile firms increases their ability to transform product and process innovations into business activities having superior business performance (Lewin and Massini 2003). The period from domestic establishment to initial foreign market entry is often 3 years or less (Autio et al. 2000; McDougall & Oviatt 2000; Rennie 1993).

It was becoming clear that research in the field of international entrepreneurship was to be rich in opportunity (Oviatt & McDougall 2003). The field is very broad; many important and interesting research questions have been explored, and many more existing theories are still to be discovered and investigated. In an article discussing the early state of the field in international entrepreneurial analysis, researchers Giamartino et al. (1993, p.37) stated, "In sum, the entrepreneurship field stands poised to more fully integrate an international focus into the research, teaching, and practice of venture creation and growth."

We propose that successful international new ventures exhibit four basic elements. As they usually suffer from a poverty of resources, they internalize a minimal proportion of their assets (Element 1) and focus on less costly governance mechanisms (Element 2) such as network structures, to control a greater percentage of vital resources than mature organizations would. We further propose that they gain foreign location advantages from private knowledge that they possess or produce (Element 3), and make it sustainable through one or more means of protection-imperfect imitating, licensing, networking, and using direct means, such as patents (Element 4) (Oviatt & McDougall 2005). Even in today's post-millennium era, adept business researchers are still engrossed in studying the international entrepreneurial enigma:

In spring 2004, the Wall Street Journal described what seemed to be a relatively new phenomenon called the micro-multinational; a company that from its inception is based in the US but maintains a less-costly skilled work force abroad (Grimes 2004; Oviatt & McDougall 2005).

Knight and Cavusgil (2004) argue, however, that the phenomenon of the 'born global' entrepreneurial firm, or firms that are founded from the very beginning of company formation to be international in nature, is not really a new concept: Take the issue of 'born global' firms, an area of growing concern to IB scholars (Knight & Cavusgil 2004). The phenomenon of firms that initiate a process of internationalization almost immediately after they have been established, and grow their global operations very rapidly thereafter, is generally assumed to be a new one. In fact, thousands of companies with compelling resemblances to such 'born global' firms were created in the nineteenth century. In the business history literature, they are known as 'free-standing firms', a term coined by Wilkins (1988) to describe the numerous European firms (in particular) that were established with the primary intention of pursuing international investment opportunities. The creation of such firms slowed after 1914, and stopped almost entirely after 1929 (Jones & Khanna 2006).

Wilkins (1970), and Oviatt and McDougall (1994), agree that international new ventures have existed for centuries. They cite examples such as the famous London based East India Company of the 1600's, and the American specialized cotton traders of the early 19th century (Chandler 1977). The main difference, however, between these historical international firms and the entrepreneurial INVs of today is in the focus of interest; historically this focus has been placed upon multinational enterprises (MNEs) that have developed over a long time from large, mature, and integrated enterprises (Chandler 1986). Oviatt and McDougall (1994) further indicate that this primary focus on the large MNEs have essentially obscured the existence of the 'born global' smaller international new ventures.

In contrast to the traditional pattern of firms that operate in the domestic market for many years and gradually evolve into international trade (e.g., Johanson & Vahlne 1977), these early adopters of internationalization begin with a global view of their markets, and develop the capabilities needed to achieve their international goals at or near the firm's founding (Knight & Cavusgil 2004).

Among the researchers who subscribe to the viability and relative significance of the international entrepreneur and the international new venture (INV) theory, an operational definition of this 'business maverick' was needed.

International entrepreneurship is the discovery, enactment, evaluation, and exploitation of opportunities - across national borders - to create future goods and services. It follows, therefore, that the scholarly field of international entrepreneurship examines and compares - across national borders - how, by whom, and with what effects those opportunities are acted upon (McDougall & Oviatt 2003).

This current characterization of the IE points out that certain qualities are required in order to make firms truly entrepreneurial. These defining qualities include innovativeness, creativeness, and risk taking (Zahra 2005). As this portrayal also indicates, the *by whom* and *how* elements of international entrepreneurship are of great import; international entrepreneurship must have in its base structure two vital parts: (1) opportunities; and (2) individuals who strive to take advantage of them (Oviatt & McDougall 2005).

Several important research studies have been conducted on entrepreneurial opportunities, and the individuals who seize and exploit them (Baker et al. 2005). An interesting observation is that some entrepreneurs may discover INV opportunities without actively searching for them; many IEs are simply at the right place at the right time when the opportunity arises, and they possess the needed knowledge and network contacts to successfully implement the stumbled-upon venture (Kirzner 2000; Baker et al. 2003). This requires the individual clearly recognize the opportunity as viable, and the IE must be able to innovate boldly and regularly even though the INV strategy will entail considerable risks (Miller & Friesen 1982).

As stated by Zahra (2005), where opportunities exist in the environment, the successful and innovative entrepreneurs are more alert than others in spotting, recognizing, and exploiting these opportunities.

Political, institutional, and cultural factors also play a role when an IE is considering opportunities presented; when the possible or probable effects from these factors are weighed in relation to acceptance of the opportunity, the IE's evaluation of the cost of abandoning (or adding to) their current undertakings with an alternative one must be thoroughly considered (Baker et al. 2005). INV creation or expansion may involve serious risks, including political instability in the global marketplace, expropriation, social unrest, fluctuating exchange rates, poor infrastructures, host government regulations, differing language, norms, religion, and unfamiliar legal systems (Zacharakis 1997).

Innovation is particularly used by entrepreneurs to increase their chances for a successful venture (Schumpeter 1942). By creating or exploiting an invention, process, or technology the international entrepreneur leverages the INV success on the ability to innately innovate problem solutions that might otherwise stymie traditional growth businesses. New product-market development in "born-global" innovative companies seems fluid and dynamic; often continued growth is a constant process of situational redefinition resulting in improvements in both products and procedures in the competitive environment (Utterback and Abernathy 1975).

Innovating firms develop their own unique knowledge and resultant capabilities that engender organizational performance. Whereas larger, long-established firms usually experience substantial bureaucratization that hinders their innovative activities, smaller or younger firms are more flexible, less bureaucratic, and generally enjoy internal conditions that encourage innovativeness (Knight & Cavusgil 2004; Lewin & Massini 2003; Penrose 1959; Schumpeter 1942).

Knowledge gained about the markets, competition, suppliers and customers offers important clues about new opportunities in foreign markets, new markets to enter, new systems to develop, new products to offer, and new ways of organizing INVs' own operations (Zahra 2005).

Thus, it is also apparent that *timing* of the new international venture is a pre-requisite for entrepreneurial success; further, a *window of opportunity* exists for a temporal period when decisions and actions pertaining to the opportunity must be made by the entrepreneur (Kreiser et al. 2002). During this critical time, essential project foundations are laid that will enhance the chances for a successful undertaking. As a prerequisite to the opportunity, timing, and execution of the venture, another important requirement - the inherent venture implementation *know-how* - must be possessed by the entrepreneur so as to lead the venture formulation and construct development toward a desired positive resolve (Geva-May 2004). Without this substantial knowledge, the value of opportunity timing is diminished and the new venture opportunity is seriously bound. Lacking sufficient knowledge about foreign markets and operations is another major obstacle to a successful INV (Fernandez & Nieto, 2006; Johanson & Vahlne 1977).

Along with venture timing, the characterizations of *'who'* might possess the inherent qualities necessary become international entrepreneurs has been noteworthy of research (Zacharakis 1997). Because IE INV startups are typically resource constrained (Jarillo 1989; Spann 1990; Stinchcombe 1965; Vesper 1990), they must use any and all resources they can muster in order to successfully enter and sustain in an international market. Many IE ventures consist of partners, each of who brings to the venture some part of indispensable knowledge required for the operation (Zacharakis 1997). Oviatt and McDougall (1994) term this as *hybrid entry strategies*. These confederates can, in tandem, help leverage their resources together and increase the INV's viability and market sustainability.

Whereas larger, long-established firms usually experience substantial bureaucratization that hinders their innovative activities, smaller or younger firms are more flexible, less bureaucratic, and generally enjoy internal conditions that encourage innovativeness (Knight & Cavusgil 2004; Lewin & Massini 2003; Penrose 1959; Schumpeter 1942).

The *where* element of the IE definition may be one of the most important and difficult for the international entrepreneur. Nations vary widely in their capacity to support different types of economic activity (Porter 1990), as well as in the varieties of market and institutional voids (Khanna & Palepu 1997) that may present (or limit) opportunities to potential entrepreneurs (Baker et al. 2005).

To the international entrepreneur, tax and fiscal policies of a proposed INV location are very important in the determination of where to locate the business venture and can vary widely across nations and affect anticipated benefits (Baker et al. 2005). Taxes, or lack thereof, can directly increase or diminish expected profits. In addition, international country policies that pertain to economic factors such as government subsidies, tax breaks and depreciation rules can be leveraged by the entrepreneur in the determination of where to strategically place the business venture. In the same vein, Baker et al. (2005) indicate that the institutional and cultural features of a nation influence these profit reference points by affecting the amounts and types of benefits that an entrepreneur can expect to receive. According to their study, these economic benefits must be weighed from a feasibility viewpoint, and a comparison made of the options available so the IE can correctly determine the costs of abandoning current circumstances verses the costs of continued venture pursuit.

A criticism of the McDougall and Oviatt (2003) operational definition is 'why' an entrepreneur should decide to undertake such an involved and risk-laden circumstance (Zacharakis 1997). As to why born-globals internationalize early, Knight and Cavusgil (2004) state that very little research attempts an explanation. They also indicate that almost no empirical research has examined the motivational forces which drive the superior international performance of these young, highly entrepreneurial international companies.

There has been very little empirical research aimed at uncovering the actual bundles of capabilities that characterize truly innovative firms, as well as the causal link between the possession of particular types of knowledge, organizational routines, and superior performance (Lewin & Massini 2003; Massini et al. 2003; Knight & Cavusgil 2004).

Some factors that seem to motivate IEs to seek international expansion includes a maturing US market for the product or service (Namiki 1988), stiff foreign competition within the U.S. market (Hazard & Yoffie 1989), and conditions present in foreign market that are favorable to the new international venture (Aharoni 1966; Hymer 1960; Simpson 1973).

In a reflective article pertaining to the previous research made in international business research, Wright and Ricks (1994) indicated that, in addition to research in the areas of international information systems, international alliances and coalitions, and environmental concerns of business, the field of international entrepreneurship was an emerging thrust of international business research.

Most of the international business research done to date can be placed fairly easily into one of two clearly definable functional categories: (1) it involves the study of a particular problem area with little or no regard to how things differ from country to country (or culture to culture); or (2) it focuses on comparisons between countries (comparative management) and/or cultures (cross-cultural management) (Wright & Ricks 1994).

The '*how*' element pertaining to the IE definition, according to Knight and Cavusgil (2004), is driven by two key trends that have allowed international entrepreneurs to successfully create INVs on such a large scale. The first trend, as these researchers suggest, is to be demonstrated with the increasing globalization of the business environment via international sourcing, production outsourcing, and global marketing. The second trend can be seen via global technological advances. Widespread diffusion of e-mail, the Internet, and related technologies has made internationalization a more viable and cost-effective option (Knight & Cavusgil 2004).

Knowledge is among the most important resources for an IE to draw upon, and the integration of the INV's specialized knowledge is the essence of organizational capabilities (Conner & Prahalad 1996; Dierickx & Cool 1989; Grant 1996; Leonard-Barton 1992; Nelson & Winter 1982; Solow 1957; Knight & Cavusgil 2004). Especially regarding international business, knowledge provides particular advantages that facilitate foreign market entry and operations (Kogut & Zander 1993).

When further defining *how* an IE with limited resources is to develop such a venture, a 'strategic network' of alliances are formed within the structure of the international new venture, and that of an alliance, however loosely coupled, works to the advantage of the INV formation and continued operation (Child & Faulkner 1998).

Alliances may be concluded for transaction-cost reasons, but networks never are. Networks generally exist for reasons stemming from resource-dependency theory - that is, one network member provides one function which is complementary to and synergistic with the differing contribution of other members of the network. Although costs enter into the calculus of who to admit and persevere with as network members, the existence of the network, and the loose bonding implied by it, emphasize autonomy and choice, in contrast to the more deterministic governance structure and stable static equilibrium applied to alliance theory by transaction cost theorists (Child & Faulkner 1998).

Considering the limited resources of entrepreneurial businesses, entrepreneurs may lack that strong network, especially in the international domain (Zacharakis 1997). As such, INV firms often find themselves with other allies that are familiar with the risks and the rewards of operating in the selected area of venture, even though they may not be familiar with one another. In this case, the IE must choose carefully the parties to ally with, and to insure they will possess necessary skills, be able to consistently perform, and will facilitate the venture to a successful resolution (Zacharakis 1997). If the parties involved are from the country where the

INV is located, different cultural values affect individual cognition which in turn results in different behavior (Abramson et al. 1993; Busenitz & Lau 1996). Building relationships and gaining access to existing networks can help to shorten and expedite international new venture's learning (Zahra, 2005). Hiring locals is another way of gaining access to tacit knowledge about cultural norms and their implications, contributing to INVs' ability to build and gain a competitive advantage.

The level of complexity facing entrepreneurs in making decisions is generally much greater than that of other managers and decision makers. Entrepreneurs, especially in the formative stages of their organizations, do not have the luxury of becoming expert decision makers in a specific area (Gilmore & Kazanjian 1989). They must make decisions on everything from a firm's competitive strategy to hiring personnel to technical product development issues. These numerous and often interrelated decisions create a very complex decision-making context, a context where simplifying biases and heuristics can have a great deal of utility in enabling entrepreneurs to make decisions in a timely manner (Busenitz & Lau 1996).

According to Zahra (2005), it is easy to understate the subtle and profound role of national cultures, history and geography. These variables interact in important ways that define the nature and magnitude of opportunities that exist in a country or region. With founder-owners in control, new knowledge does not have to struggle for management's attention and acceptance.

Data Preparation and Collection

The current paper describes the case study of an American international new venture formed in Thailand. The case methodology was used since much of the collected data came directly from the experiences of the owners themselves. As discussed by Rouse and Daellenbach (1999), case methodology is also helpful in generating sensitive, confidential or consequential data (Coviello 2006).

That is, they had fewer than 10 employees, were less than 6 years of age, and had entered their first foreign market within 3 years of conception. Consequently, they met the size, age and export criteria used by McDougall and Oviatt (2003). Cases also needed to meet the more general definition of an INV, where, from inception, the new venture seeks to derive 'significant competitive advantage from the use of resources and sale of outputs in multiple countries' (Coviello 2006).

Data collection involved administering two surveys of inductive interviews, and data were then analyzed by the study's author. The first interview was conducted with the owners/founders/managers responsible for general management. These were the primary informants for topics regarding business pre-conception, network dynamics involving business creation and the exploitation of social capital during business formation. These individuals were chosen because of their direct and hands-on experience with the firm's evolution.

Company owners, managers, and such are considered appropriate because they typically have knowledge of and involvement in the new venture's various relationships (McCartan-Quinn & Carson 2003; Barringer et al. 2005; Coviello 2006).

The starting point for the interview pertained to initial business idea conception for the international new venture. Since the INV owners were American and spoke fluent English, the author administered the interview to them. The interview questions and responses given were audio taped, and then transcribed for analysis.

The second interview targeted the Thai workers currently employed in the venture. Among other topics investigated, the employee attitudes pertaining to general work ethics, opinions regarding the current work environment and the sentiment of working in the foreign INV were qualitatively recorded.

Organizational culture plays an important role in an employee's level of diversity openness as it both shapes the meanings and actions of its members (Ashkanasy et al. 2000), as well as being shaped by its members, through their interpersonal relationships at work (Ancona et al. 1999). The learned common assumptions underlying an organization's culture are 'the ultimate causal determinant of feelings, attitudes, espoused values and overt behaviors (Schein 1990; Hartel 2004).

All of the employees interviewed were Thai, so the interview was administered by a bilingual Thai/English associate interviewer. The interview questions and responses were also recorded on audio tape, and then transcribed verbatim by the bilingual associate for analysis.

As recommended by Pettigrew et al. (2001), the language of 'what, who, where, why, when and how' was used to guide the research protocol for the interviews. The transcriptions were used to recreate the biographic history and identify the situational network dynamics present in the interview content.

Biographic histories are a practical way to study the process of entrepreneurial behavior, because chronological events can be used as stepping stones in the search for patterns over time (Pettigrew et al. 2001; Hurmerinta-Peltomaki 2003; Coviello 2006)

The biographic history of the INV allows for a detailed chronology of events which acted as a catalyst in the venture formation and development. In addition to events, the biographic history allows for identification of key relationships, social capital used and transferred, and other key network dynamic components implicated in the venture creation and development.

Data Analysis

In analyzing the results from the interview with the owners of the INV, responses from the questions were grouped into selected categories which followed Kazanjian's (1988) four-stage framework:

Stage 1: Concept generation, resource acquisition, tech development.
Stage 2: Production-related start-up and commercialization.
Stage 3: Sales growth and organizational issues.
Stage 4: Stability and profitability.

Stage 1: Owner responses relevant to the framework (concept generation) were as follows:
1. August 1st – Inception date: determine type of business desired;
2. Research Thailand labor force, wage labor laws;
3. Determine estimate of overhead when doing business in Thailand;
a. Develop the business plan: (a) Profit and loss sheet; (b) Work flow, proposed schedule; (c) Benefits of retaining US company status (Amity Treaty company); (d) Design communication and computer networks for both verbal and data communication from Thailand to the US;
4. Conduct a meeting with MBA CEO (Ferguson) to pitch business plan and proposal.

Stage 2: Regarding production-related startup, the following issues were indicated from the interview by the owners:
1. Secure the RMBS (Thailand) office location;
2. Create US LLC company for tax purposes and as a business entity to receive and hold money in the US bank;
3. Find a legitimate and competent Thai legal firm to create initial documents required for Thai LTD Amity Treaty Corporation;
4. Obtain a business loan from US local bank to initially finance new venture (use business plan created earlier);

5. Develop a possible working time frame for new Thai LTD company development and association with the US LLC company;
6. Make travel plans for business partner (who is also to act as General Manager);
7. Get bids and estimate from Thai companies for remodeling of new LTD facility – carpet, glass tinting, window blinds, office desks and chairs, computers, networking gear;
8. Modify new facility electrical requirements (new breakers, wiring) to support over 12 computers, monitors, batter backup units, network routers, ADSL modems, etc.

Stage 3: Sales and organization issues:
1. Obtain a supporting medical billing outsourcing for specialty bill coding which will not be implemented upon startup of LTD;
2. Research arrangements for friends and family to care for personal affairs while away;
3. Proof documents from Thai law firm and submit documents to the Thai government;
4. Purchase remodeling fixtures, carpet, blinds, computers, printers, network gear, etc. from previous bids received;
5. Finalize outsourcing contract between MBA and RMBS (Thailand) (3 year contract);
6. Locate living quarters near new company office (within 10-minute walking distance);
7. Hire Office Manager and Supervisor positions (both Thai employees);
8. Perform final MBA company modifications for LTD company access and information/data transfer;
9. Create new LTD policy procedure manual and employee manual (written in English) and have them translated into Thai;
10. Finalize contract with specialty medical coding outsourcing company;
11. Install new furnishings, carpet, blinds, computers, computer network;
12. Coordinate getting personal items from the US packed and shipped to Thailand;
13. Thai Office Manager to start purchasing general office supplies;
14. Perform computer network, routers and ADSL modem installation; create and test data link with the MBA site in the US;
15. Research best method of transferring money to and from Thailand (initially there will be no Thai bank account);
16. Direct Thai law firm to begin process for a Thai work permit for the General Manager;
17. Finalize arrangements for handling USA personal affairs;

18. Travel to Thailand and move into selected residence.

Stage 4: Stability and profit issues were defined by the owners in the interview as:
1. Advertising employee positions needed: (a) must live within walking distance (10 minutes) from the new office; (b) must be a Thai national; (c) proficiency in reading English required (speaking not a requirement); (d) typing ability of at least 30 English words per minute; (e) effective use of 10-key calculator;
2. Interviewing and selection process of potential employees;
3. Perform 3-week employee training session;
4. Start live Nov 1st – **90 days** from inception;

In the analysis of the Thai employee interviews, responses were generally contained in defining the work attitudes and employee-supervisor relationship in three main areas:

Area 1: Strengths of the American owners/supervisors
Area 2: Weaknesses of the American owners/supervisors
Area 3: Behaviors that seem to frustrate the American owners/supervisors

Area 1: Strengths of the supervisors; Thai responses were generalized as:
1. Willingness to understand the Thai culture and accommodate differences;
2. Openness by the supervisors to talk about the employee's work performance;
3. Strong work ethic and very knowledgeable in the business operations;
4. Politeness and reasonableness regarding subordinate's issues;
5. Seeks group commitment and decisive in group policy and procedures;
6. Good utilization of resources (equipment, supplies, work environment);
7. Supportive in employee efforts, as all employees seem treated equal;
8. Not afraid of confrontation regarding business decisions.
In summary, the perceived strengths of the American owners/supervisors by the Thai employees indicated the supervisors were:
1. Decisive in their approach to business;
2. Exhibited a high degree of professionalism with both employees and clients;
3. Utilized good communication skills for cross-cultural understanding;
4. Demonstrated a results-oriented approach to achieve a high capacity output from the employees;

5. Used straight-forward business direction so employees know what is expected;
6. Minimal personal involvement regarding the employee's personal affairs.

Area 2: Thai interview responses to weaknesses of the American supervisors included:
1. Were 'bossy' and jumped to conclusions easily;
2. Underestimated the abilities of the staff to complete job assignments correctly;
3. Misinterpreted the Thai employee's communications;
4. Lacked understanding in specific Thai cultural work attitudes;
5. Lacked feelings of trust among the supervisors and the employees;
6. Seemed 'distant' at times, somewhat impersonal.

Area 3: Thai behaviors that frustrated the American supervisors included:
1. Being too compromising or weak in defending the company policy;
2. Not being punctual for work or appointments;
3. Talked too much during working hours with other Thai employees;
4. Used the cell phone for personal calls during work hours;
5. Unable to express the employee's reasoning;
6. Indirect when asked explicit and definite questions;
7. Appearance of irresponsibility regarding work completion;
8. Not following through on work as required;
9. Non-completion of assigned work in the time scheduled.

Conclusions

In this paper, a particular INV case study was used to indicate some basic qualities and concepts required for an initial born-global startup. The study of international entrepreneurship and the international new venture is a relatively new area of research in business. Within the last 25 years, this field has seemed to develop into an exciting and complex phenomenon. Some ventures, such as the born-global companies, start their existence intended on international or global commerce. Current theories pertaining to network dynamics, social capital, and cross-cultural interactions help to explain certain aspects of these business ventures, but much research in the area is still needed.

References

Abramson, N.R., Lane, H.W., Nagai, T. & Takagi, H. 1993. A comparison of Canadian and Japanese cognitive styles: Implications for management interaction. *Journal of International Business Studies.* 24(3):575-587

Aharoni, Y. 1966. *The Foreign Investment Process.* Boston: Harvard Business School

Ancona, D., Kochan, T., Scully, M., Van Maanen, J. & Westney, E.D. 1999. *Managing for the Future: Organizational Behavior & Processes.* Cincinnati: South-Western

Ashkanasy, N.M., Wilderom, C.P.M. & Peterson, M.F. 2000. *Handbook of Organizational Culture & Climate.* Thousand Oaks: Sage

Autio, E., Sapienza, H. & Almeida, J. 2000. Effects of age at entry, knowledge intensity, and imitability on international growth. *Academy of Management Journal.* 43(5):909-924

Baker, T., Gedajlovic, E. & Lubatkin, M. 2005. A Framework for Comparing Entrepreneurship Processes across Nations. *Journal of International Business Studies.* 36(5):492+

Baker, T., Miner, A. & Eesley, D. 2003. Improvising firms: Bricolage, account giving and improvisational competencies in the founding process. *Research Policy.* 32:255-276

Barringer, B.R., Jones, F.F. & Neubaum, D.O. 2005. A quantitative content analysis of the characteristics of rapid-growth firms and their founders. *Journal of Business Venturing.* 20(5):663-687

Busenitz, L.W. & Lau, C.M. 1996. A cross-cultural cognitive model of new venture creation. Entrepreneurship Theory and Practice. 20(4):25-39

Chandler, A.D. 1977. *The Visible Hand.* Cambridge: Belknap

—. 1986. The evolution of modern global competition. In M.E.Porter (ed.). *Competition in Global Industries.* Boston: Harvard Business School. 405-448

Child, J. & Faulkner, D. 1998. *Strategies of Cooperation: Managing Alliances, Networks, and Joint Ventures.* New York: Oxford University

Cole, A.H. 1968. Meso-economics: A contribution from entrepreneurial history. *Explorations in Entrepreneurial History.* 6(1):3-33

Conner, K. & Prahalad, C.K. 1996. A resource-based theory of the firm: Knowledge versus opportunism. *Organization Science.* 7(5):477-501

Coviello, N.E. 2006. The Network Dynamics of International New Ventures. *Journal of International Business Studies.* 37(5):713+

Dierickx, I. & Cool, K. 1989. Asset stock accumulation and sustainability of competitive advantage. *Management Science.* 35(12):1504-1510

Fernandez, Z. & Nieto, M. J. 2006. Impact of Ownership on the International Involvement of SMEs. *Journal of International Business Studies.* *37*(3):340+

Gartner. W.B. 1985. A conceptual framework for describing the phenomenon of new venture creation. *Academy of Management Review.* 10:696-706

Geva-May, I. 2004. Riding the Wave of Opportunity: Termination in Public Policy. *Journal of Public Administration Research and Theory.* *14*(3):309+

Giamartino, G.A., McDougall, P.P. & Bird, B.J. 1993. International entrepreneurship: The state of the field. *Entrepreneurship Theory and Practice*, 18:37-41

Grant, R.M. 1996. Prospering in dynamically competitive environments: organizational capability as knowledge integration. *Organization Science.* 7(4):375-387

Grimes, A. 2004. Venture firms seek start-ups that outsource. *The Wall Street Journal.* 243(2):B1-B2

Hartel, C.E. 2004. Towards a Multicultural World: Identifying Work Systems, Practices and Employee Attitudes That Embrace Diversity. *Australian Journal of Management.* *29*(2):189+

Hazard, H.A. & Yoffie, D.B. 1989. *New Theories of International Trade.* Harvard Business School. Case 9-390-001

Hurmerinta-Peltomaki, L. 2003. Time and internationalization: Theoretical challenges set by rapid internationalization. *Journal of International Entrepreneurship.* 1(2):217-236

Hymer, S. 1960. *The International Operations of National Firms: A Study of Direct Investment.* Unpublished doctoral dissertation. Boston: MIT

Jarillo, J.C. 1989. Entrepreneurship and growth: The strategic use of external resources. *Journal of Business Venturing.* 4:133-147

Johanson, J. & Vahlne, J.E. 1977. The internationalization process of the firm: a model of knowledge development and increasing foreign market commitments. *Journal of International Business Studies.* 8(1):23-32

Jones, G., & Khanna, T. 2006. Bringing History (Back) into International Business. *Journal of International Business Studies.* *37*(4):453+

Kazanjian, R.K. 1988. Relation of dominant problems to stages of growth in technology-based new ventures. *Academy of Management Journal.* 31(2):259-279

Khanna, T. & Palepu, K. 1997. Why focused strategies may be wrong for emerging markets. *Harvard Business Review.* 75(4):41-49

Kirzner, I.M. 2000. *The Driving Force of the Market: Essays in Austrian Economics.* London: Routledge

Knight, F. 1921. *Risk, Uncertainty and Profit.* Boston: Houghton Mifflin.

Knight, G.A. & Cavusgil, S.T. 2004. Innovation, organization capabilities, and the born-global firm. *Journal of International Business Studies.* 35(2):124-141

Kogut, B. & Zander, U. 1993. Knowledge of the firm and the evolutionary theory of the multinational corporation. *Journal of International Business Studies.* 24(4):625-645

Kreiser, P.M., Marino, L.D. & Weaver, K.M. 2002. Assessing the psychometric properties of the entrepreneurial orientation scale: A multi-country analysis. *Entrepreneurship: Theory and Practice.* 26(4):71+

Lado, A.A. & Vozikis, G.S. 1996. Transfer of technology to promote entrepreneurship in developing countries: An integration and proposed framework. *Entrepreneurship: Theory and Practice.* 21(2):55

Leonard-Barton, D. 1992. Core capabilities and core rigidities: A paradox in managing new product development. *Strategic Management Journal.* 13:111-126

Lewin, A.Y. & Massini, S. 2003. Knowledge creation and organizational capabilities of innovating and imitating firms. in H.Tsoukas & N.Mylonopoulos (eds.). *Organizations as Knowledge Systems.* Basingstoke: Palgrave

Massini, S., Lewin, A.Y. & Greve, H.E. 2003. Innovators and imitators: Organizational reference groups and adoption of organizational routines. (unpublished manuscript)

McCartan-Quinn, D. & Carson, D. 2003. Issues which impact upon marketing in the small firm. *Small Business Economics.* 21(2):201-213

McDougall, P.P. 1989. International versus domestic entrepreneurship: New venture strategic behavior and industry structure. *Journal of Business Venturing.* 4:387-399

McDougall, P. & Oviatt, B. 2000. International entrepreneurship: The intersection of two research paths. *Academy of Management Journal.* 43(5):902-906

McDougall, P.P. & Oviatt, B.M. 2003. *Some Fundamental Issues in International Entrepreneurship.* Retrieved April 27, 2008 from http://www.usasbe.org

McDougall, P.P., Shane, S. & Oviatt, B.M. 1994. Explaining the formation of international new ventures: The limits of theories from international business research. *Journal of Business Venturing.* 9:469-487

Miller, D. & Friesen, P.H. 1982. Innovation in conservative and entrepreneurial firms: Two models of strategic momentum. *Strategic Management Journal.* 3:1-25

Morrow, J.F. 1988. International entrepreneurship: A new growth opportunity. *New Management.* 3:59-61

Namiki, N. 1988. Export strategy for small business. *Journal of Small Business Management.* 26(2):33-37

Nelson, R. & Winter, S. 1982. *An Evolutionary Theory of Economic Change.* Cambridge: Belknap

Oviatt, B.M., & McDougall, P.P. 1994. Toward a Theory of International New Ventures. *Journal of International Business Studies.* 25(1):45+

Oviatt, B.M., & McDougall, P.P. 2003. Some fundamental issues in international entrepreneurship. *Entrepreneurship: Theory and Practice.* 27(2): 342+

Oviatt, B.M., & McDougall, P.P. 2005. Defining international entrepreneurship and modeling the speed of internationalization. *Entrepreneurship: Theory and Practice.* 29(5):537+

Penrose, E. 1959. *The Theory of the Growth of the Firm.* London: Basil Blackwell

Pettigrew, A.M., Woodman, R.W. & Cameron, K.S. 2001. Studying organizational change and development: Challenges for future research. *Academy of Management Journal.* 44(4):697-713

Porter, M.E. 1990. *The Competitive Advantage of Nations.* New York: Free Press

Rennie, M. 1993. Born global. *McKinsey Quarterly.* (4):45-52

Rouse, M.J. & Daellenbach, U.S. 1999. Rethinking research methods for the resource-based perspective: Isolating sources of sustainable competitive advantage. *Strategic Management Journal.* 20(5):487-494

Rumelt, R. P. 1987. Theory, strategy and entrepreneurship. in D.J.Teece (Ed). The Competitive Challenge: Strategies for Industrial Innovation and Renewal. Cambridge: Ballinger. 137-157

Schein, E.H. 1990. Organizational culture. *American Psychologist.* 45:109-19

Schumpeter, J. 1942. *Capitalism, Socialism, and Democracy.* New York: Harper & Brothers

Simpson, C. L. 1973. *The Export Decision: An Interview Study of the Decision Process in Tennessee Manufacturing Firms.* Unpublished doctoral dissertation. Atlanta: Georgia State University

Solow, R.M. 1957. Technical change and the aggregate production function. *Review of Economics and Statistics.* 39(February):312-320

Spann, M. S. 1990. *Resource Acquisition Strategies of Entrepreneurs.* Unpublished doctoral dissertation. Knoxville: University of Tennessee.

Stevenson, H.H., Roberts, M.J. & Grousbeck, H.A. 1985. *New Business Ventures and the Entrepreneur.* Homewood: Irwin

Stinchcombe, A.L. 1965. Social structure and organizations. In J.March (Ed.). *Handbook of Organizations.* Chicago: Rand McNally. 142-193

Utterback, J.M. & Abernathy, W.J. 1975. A dynamic model of process and product innovation. *Omega.* 3(6):639-656

Vesper, K.C. 1990. New Venture Strategies. (Revised Ed.). New Jersey: Prentice Hall

Wilkins, M. 1970. *The Emergence of Multinational Enterprise.* Cambridge: Harvard University

Wilkins, M. 1988. The free-standing company, 1870-1914: An important type of British foreign direct investment. *Economic History Review.* 41(2):259-285

Wright, R.W. & Ricks, D.A. 1994. Trends in international business research: Twenty-five years later. *Journal of International Business Studies.* 25(4):687-713

Zacharakis, A. 1997. Entrepreneurial entry into foreign markets: A transaction cost perspective. *Entrepreneurship: Theory and Practice.* 21(3):23+

Zahra, S.A. 2005. A theory of international new ventures: A decade of research. *Journal of International Business Studies.* 36(1):20+

Zahra, S.A. & George, G. 2002. International entrepreneurship: The current status of the field and future research agenda. In M.A.Hitt, R.D.Ireland, S.M.Camp & D.L.Sexton (Eds). *Strategic Entrepreneurship: Creating a New Mindset.* Oxford: Blackwell. 255-288

Chapter Five

Reform of Sales Management and Evolution of the Role of *Guanxi* in China

Mark Speece, Jonathan Lee and Jun Han

Abstract

An old case study of B2B sales in the Shaanxi's machine tool industry shows an early stage of reform of the sales function in China. Without foreign influence, many State-Owned Enterprises (SOEs) nevertheless moved to professionalize sales. Strongly reforming SOEs began building sales forces of qualified, trained professionals. Customers themselves reported that prior guanxi was not necessary when they encountered such reps, and began placing trial orders. Good service led to bigger shifts of volume to these professional reps, who gradually developed guanxi in the course of interaction with their customers. This new guanxi served mainly to facilitate information flow in a consultative sales role.

Introduction

Sales management in modern China was traditionally quite poor, as the sales function was almost irrelevant under central planning. Transition to a market economy over the past few decades has forced change. Originally, foreign influence introduced modern sales management in coastal areas, but even in the absence of foreign competitive pressure, some SOEs moved early to modernize sales. We report on an old case study from a decade ago, which clearly shows the basic issues in a part of China where there was very little foreign influence at the time. We follow up with discussion showing how these trends have continued, fostering professionalization of the sales function. As personal selling evolves in China, the role of *guanxi* (roughly, connections) in the sales function is shifting.

In industrial markets, relationship marketing has increasingly been recognized as an effective way to develop long-term sales. Most observers have stressed that relationship marketing involves a long-term and complex relationship, not simply or only a series of transactions (see, for example, Harker 1999; Weitz & Bradford 1999). Some authors have seen *guanxi* as a traditional, Chinese form of relationship marketing (Wong & Chan 1999). Most, though, maintain that *guanxi* is essentially a social concept, although it does permeate business transactions at all levels, and business takes on strong social elements (Arias 1998; Luo 1997; Tsang 1998).

Nevertheless, this earlier work often pointed out the importance of *guanxi* in business, because traditional business followed social networks. More recently, some observers have pointed out negative consequences from the strong influence of *guanxi* (Chen & Chen 2009; Luo 2008). Such critique is undoubtedly valid to some extent, but there is also a very positive role for *guanxi*. For example, Zhuang et al. (2010) show that *guanxi* reduces use of coercive power in marketing channels, increases use of non-coercive power, and generally reduces channel conflict. One key 'non-coercive power' element is information, which is especially critical in sales. Early on, Weitz and Bradford (1999) suggested that interpersonal communication between sales rep and customer plays a key role in developing relationships. Information exchange is a key element in a *guanxi* system, and there would be little information flow if parties did not have a strong *guanxi* relationship (Arias 1998; Wong 1998).

We show these issues in an early stage of professionalization of sales by re-examining a case study on B2B customer perceptions of SOE sales reps in the machine tool industry of Shaanxi province (Han 1999). Sales management was just beginning to receive strong attention in both trade and academic literature in China, as some companies became serious about making the transition to the market economy (Gan 1998; Shao 1998; Wang 1998a, 1998b; Xu & Cai 1998; Zhang & Xie 1992). Generally, enterprises with some foreign participation had started adapting most readily, bringing in foreign ideas about selling and sales management. But top management in some SOEs had also begun to adopt some modern forms of sales management (Wu & Speece 1998).

This project showed that SOE customers of the Shaanxi SOE suppliers preferred dealing with professional sales reps, even without prior *guanxi*, to dealing with traditional sales reps. Of course, traditional reps were relatively low status, and had little *guanxi* at the levels needed for deal-making, but reforming customer companies were developing more modern forms of management, which shifted procurement responsibility downward to purchasing managers and other decision influencers directly involved in using the machinery. Thus, professional reps could get in the door, and over time, guild up *guanxi*. The role of *guanxi* shifted to one of facilitating information flow to help sales reps develop forms of consultative selling characteristic of true relationship marketing.

Methodology

The target population in this research was SOEs in machinery manufacturing industries and their customers in Shaanxi province. Shaanxi is an elongated interior province, bordered by Inner Mongolia on the north and Sichuan on the south. At the time of this project a decade ago, Shaanxi was representative of interior provinces which had attracted very little foreign investment. The province had negligible foreign investment (less than one-fourth of one percent of the foreign investment in the Beijing-Tianjin area, which was the third ranking area at the time, behind Guangdong Province and the Shanghai area; CSY 1997).

Among many such interior provinces, Shaanxi specifically was chosen because one of the authors had worked in the machinery industry in the province, and retained the connections necessary to gain access to companies to interview sales managers, sales reps, and customers. Such connections are often the only way to gain access to detailed information in most Chinese companies. This anticipated a point about judgment sampling in qualitative research made by Srijumpa et al. (2004, p.69), that:

"In Asia, with its strong traditions of business secrecy, judgment frequently includes an assessment of access. Working through connections and introductions is frequently the only way to gain good access at any level of companies in Asia".

There were about 55 large and medium sized SOEs which manufactured machinery in Shaanxi at the time, with a work force of about 290,000. Pilot work consisted of in-depth interviews with top management in a number of companies and the chief government officer in charge of the provincial enterprise reform office, to identify companies which were reforming strongly, partially, or very little. Managers discussed reform both in their own companies, and in other companies in the industry. Assignment of a company to one of the three categories (strong, partial, no reform) depended on consensus among the researchers, managers, and the government officer about companies which clearly showed the three different degrees of reform. Those companies for which we were unable to get agreement were excluded from further consideration in this study.

Three companies in each of the three categories were selected, where we could get the most access and cooperation, for a total of nine companies.

Within each company, in-depth interviews were conducted with the sales manager, and several separate group interviews were held with three to five sales reps. The interviews covered a wide range of sales force operation, not only recruiting and training, though we report mainly on recruiting and training issues here to demonstrate that reforming SOEs were building professional sales forces. Interviews with the sales managers also covered rep performance. It is also critical to consider customer feedback in evaluating sales rep performance (Lambert et al. 1997), and separate in-depth interviews were conducted with one major customer for each company, usually the purchasing officer, or sometimes with several people in the purchasing office. These customers were introduced by the sales managers and were among the major accounts for the SOE. Sales managers undoubtedly introduced customers who were likely to be relatively favorable; nevertheless, there were distinct differences in what customers told us by category of supplier.

Recruiting

As was noted in a study on sales management in Beijing (Wu & Speece 1998), SOEs in Shaanxi were generally unable to attract many experienced sales reps, which is why training was a key issue. All SOEs in this study relied more heavily on internal sources and new university graduates for sales reps, but the relative proportions differed by category. SOEs which had reformed at least partially generally insisted on university education, usually in technical subjects. Unreformed SOEs rarely got new reps with tertiary education, and almost all reps were internal transfers. The recruitment process was more open and more formal the more strongly the SOEs had reformed.

Strong reform SOEs did recruit internally, and HR managers tended to favor internal transfer, because the SOE did not have to deal with the government bureaucracy for internal transfers. Internally recruited reps often came from technical departments, but sometimes from marketing positions or from back-office support for the sales force. Some sales managers partially agreed with the HR preference, but for different reasons. They worried that most people hired from outside were likely to leave the SOE eventually. Such reps often regarded the SOE as a training ground where they could gain experience which would help them find a position later in a joint venture or foreign company (an issue also noted by Wu & Speece 1998).

Generally, internal recruits held a university degree. Most externally recruited reps were new university graduates. Whether internal or external, technical and product knowledge was an important criterion in selection. The strong reform SOEs tended to compete mainly on technical competence, including strong customer technical support, so they wanted their reps to have strong technical background.

Positions were announced in the local media and posted in internal bulletins. Internal applicants needed permission from their departments to apply. Sales managers said that this discouraged some from applying, as their department might have considered it disloyal to want to leave. However, the managers generally considered the ones who did apply as more forward thinking, who viewed the sales department as well-positioned for the newly developing market economy in China. Connections tended to play a substantial role in getting either internal or external applicants into the applicant pool. However, connections were not sufficient to get selected, and within the pool, the application process was fairly competitive.

Applicants sat for a written exam which tested knowledge about marketing, sales, management, and business-related legal issues. A hands-on applications exam demonstrated practical technical knowledge through solving typical technical problems. Applicants who passed these exams were interviewed, where sales managers observed appearance and personality. The final decision was the responsibility of the sales manager. However, a broad committee including top management and managers of other departments (especially HR, production, QC, training) observed the interview process, and participated in the hiring decision. Thus, while connections could get an applicant into the process, it was difficult to get hired purely on connections if an applicant was not moderately qualified and competitive relative to other applicants.

All sales reps, including old-timers from before the system was implemented, had to pass through the recruitment screening process. The old-timers may have gotten somewhat more relaxed standards in deference to their long tenure with the company, but they had to meet at least minimal qualifications and aptitude standards. If they did too badly, they were transferred out of sales. There was no strong division of the sales force among old-style vs. more modern professional selling.

Partially reformed SOEs used similar recruiting sources, but the proportion coming from internal divisions was much higher, and few reps actually come from outside. Generally, education levels were somewhat lower, also. These SOEs wanted tertiary education, but usually got recruits with a two or three-year associate degree, or from vocational schools or an open university, rather than reps with a regular, full four-year bachelor degree. While the strong reform SOEs had begun to develop sales forces where the reps had somewhat above average education compared to the general workforce, here education levels were not as high.

The recruiting process from the outside (new grads) was similar in structure, but examination and interview content was not as rigorous, and the extent of participation by different managers was not as extensive. In particular, the exam was usually more oriented toward purely theoretical knowledge, and potential recruits were often put through a training class to prep them for the exam. More attention was given to the connections network than in strong reform SOEs. Internal recruits were often simply picked on the spot by the sales manager when an unprofitable division was downsized, and may not even have faced the exam-interview process.

This recruiting process seemed to be evolving toward the same kind of process as in strongly reformed SOEs, but mainly applied to newer reps. It had not been in place as long as in the strong reform SOEs, and old-timers did not have to go through the process. Most older sales reps had entered when a new sales manager had been appointed, who brought in his own people. In other words, in the recent past, getting a rep job depended entirely on good connections with the sales manager. There would be several cohorts among these older reps, if there has been some turnover in sales managers, but they had similar profiles. Newer reps described a process which was much more competitive, rather than *guanxi* based.

Unreformed SOEs recruited almost entirely internally, with only a few newly graduated students coming in from outside. According to one manager, the state still assigns graduates to the company (all divisions, not only sales), but most of them reject the assignment and never show up. A few who were children of current employees did take positions, and they usually had lesser tertiary degrees, as in the partially reformed SOEs. Beyond state assignment, there was no formal recruitment process. Internal employees usually got the position on the strength of their connections to someone in a higher management level. There was no shortage of applicants; most considered a sales job slightly more attractive than other positions because it included an expense account and the opportunity to get out and develop the connections network. None of the recruits faced any exam or interview.

Training

Strong reform SOEs utilized internal training more frequently, but external training was given to some reps. All reps joined internal training sessions, which were organized by the SOE's own training department jointly with the sales division. Content was wide ranging, including product and technology issues, marketing and sales, legal and contract issues, accounting, computer skills, and English. Sales managers were generally most concerned about product and technology knowledge, and perceived lack of knowledge about these as the most critical problem in building a good sales force. However, most lecturers on these issues came from the production department, and there did not seem to be much attempt to look at the product/technology from a customer viewpoint.

More promising reps, who had some experience were often sent to external courses, offered by the state industry administration, universities, or sometimes overseas organizations. However, most of this sort of training was also lecture format. There seems to have been little of the more advanced sort of training methods such as case study or role playing which could give reps a little practice in application of the concepts they learned. One element, however, which distinguished these strong reform SOEs from the other two categories was recognition that continuous learning was important. Even though the methods were not very advanced, these SOEs did want their reps to continuously update their knowledge. Many of these SOEs actually had internal exams to assess knowledge about various key issues.

Partially reformed SOEs mainly trained with internal courses. The production or technology departments of the company offered lectures on product and technology issues, and internal trainers lectured on marketing and legal issues. External training was only rarely used, and then almost always only with the state industry administration training program. These SOEs were somewhat narrower in the range of knowledge they wanted reps to master. Even the concept of marketing in training focused more strongly on product issues, rather than aspects of customer orientation. These SOEs also tended to focus more strongly on new reps in their training effort. The concept of continuous learning was not well established, thus, the sales force was divided roughly into two groups, which practiced old-style selling vs. more modern selling (though not as professional as in strong reform SOEs).

Unreformed SOEs generally did not have any organized training program, other than to encourage on-the-job training which mainly consisted of following an experienced rep around and observing. They expected new reps to gain some basic knowledge of industry trends, company policy, and marketing principles mainly through self-learning. However, there was little formal attempt to actually see if reps had gained any of this knowledge. Overall, these unreformed SOEs did not seem to recognize that reps required much knowledge at all, and correspondingly, training played hardly any role at all for the sales force.

Overall, while stronger reform seemed to be introducing substantially better recruitment practices into SOEs, there did not seem to be as much impact on training practice. The more strongly reformed SOEs did certainly recognize that reps needed a wide ranging knowledge base. However, training methods were mainly lecture, focused on presenting concepts, or self-learning for actual skill acquisition. Methods which would have developed analytical skills or sales technique were not widely used. Strong reform SOEs were beginning to implement assessment techniques to determine how much reps actually knew about some elements in the knowledge base, but the methodology was not yet very sophisticated.

In assessing the training they received, many reps in strongly or partially reformed SOEs said that the topics were relevant, but that often the material was highly theoretical and not of much practical use. These reps viewed training as valuable in helping them upgrade their selling skills for better performance and for career development. They appreciated the training they got, but they wanted training methods to be improved so that they would not have to figure out how to apply concepts through trial and error. Very few reps in unreformed SOEs even recognized that training was useful – they talked a lot about the need to be good in social activities (for example, chatting, drinking, dancing, karaoke). According to most of these reps, as long as someone could socialize well, no training was needed anyway, so it did not matter if their companies did not provide any training.

Rep Satisfaction and Customer Response

As might be expected, reps themselves showed different levels of enthusiasm for their jobs. In **strong reform SOEs**, they were quite satisfied, and very motivated to do well. They viewed sales as one of the most important functions in the SOE, and they expected and received compensation well above average if they did a good job. Further, they believed that top management took sales very seriously because it was careful to select and train reps. They perceived strong support for their personal efforts to improve their incomes and living standards, and that management guarded against dragging them down with unqualified personal who wanted a free ride off of their efforts. These reps mostly applied for sales jobs because they wanted to make sales a long-term career. They rarely thought about moving to another company because they felt their own SOE gave high priority to sales and worked to make sure they could advance.

In the **partially reformed SOEs**, reps were mostly satisfied with being in sales, but they were not very satisfied with their company. These reps also wanted to make careers in sales, but they rarely talked about staying in the SOE where they currently worked, because they were less likely to perceive it as being very serious about the sales function. Some of them wanted to move to better SOEs, sometimes citing the ones we identified here as strong reform SOEs. Others talked about setting up their own independent sales agency and representing manufacturers who had failed to develop a good sales force. These reps generally viewed their current job as a training ground to practice selling skills, accumulate experience, and broaden connections, which would all be valuable when they made the move.

Reps in **unreformed SOEs** were distinctly dissatisfied with their positions. They did view the job as relatively easy compared to other jobs in their companies (reps in the other SOE categories did not view sales as easy), but they did not consider it challenging or useful in career development. These reps mostly did not view sales as a career, nor were they particularly loyal to their companies. They were likely to switch job or company (or both) if something better came along. (Something better was not likely to come along for most of these reps, as they were neither highly qualified nor highly motivated compared to reps on the other two SOE categories.)

Customer response, of course, depends on much more than only interaction with the rep, and the whole way of dealing with customers is different in the three categories of SOE. Nevertheless, satisfaction with the reps is a critical component. Customers of strong reform SOEs viewed the reps as much better than reps from other SOEs. Customers recognized the high education levels, good product knowledge, morale and enthusiasm, and selling skills among these reps. They felt that such reps were more professional, better able to adapt to customers, both on a business and a personal level, and better able to provide good after-sales service. These are the issues of credibility (expertise and trustworthiness) and availability/responsiveness, respectively, which customers generally use to evaluate sales reps (Lambert et al. 1997).

These reps were considered knowledgeable about the industry and product/technology, able to determine customer needs well, skilled at solving problems quickly, and thorough in developing internal consensus for a sale. Sometimes the purchasing manager specifically said that he appreciated the rep taking time to convince all decision influencers in other departments, as that made his job much easier. Customers also noted that such reps knew how to take advantage when the customer had time, was in a good mood, or some positive factor made it easier to interact well and in detail. They also knew when to back off if very tight deadlines made customers too busy, if they were in a bad mood, or something happened so that they did not feel like spending time with the rep at a particular time.

Relative to other sales reps, customers viewed those from strong reform SOEs as relatively younger, and lacking in a strong connections network, which is usually a disadvantage in seniority and *guanxi* conscious China. However, because of the reps' strong professionalism and ability to adapt to customers, these buyers generally preferred to deal with this kind of rep rather than others. They said that when they encountered such reps, they were usually inclined to place trial orders and see what developed. Buyers preferred to shift more volume to such reps, especially if a more traditional *guanxi* relationship developed over time. Of course, once volume got big, they would have to consider pricing a little more carefully, too. But generally, if product and price were not much different, and the rep was moderately skilled at developing traditional *guanxi* relationships after the business relationship started, most buyers were willing to shift orders to this type of rep when they could.

Customers of partially reformed SOEs were generally satisfied with rep performance on the basics, but were not as pleased with the depth of knowledge or skills. They thought these reps needed better product knowledge, and better relationship skills in a modern business sense, learning about details of customer needs and responding. They felt that the reps could understand their needs on a basic level, but did not always comprehend all the fine details. Generally, the traditional *guanxi* skills on a personal level were a little more important in these companies than in the strong reform ones, because the reps were not quite as skilled at getting in without prior *guanxi*.

Customers of the unreformed SOEs basically did not think the reps knew much. They said that product knowledge was terrible, that reps could not communicate about product or technology issues. They often just went directly to some connection in the supplier factory if they needed to deal with a supplier. Often, the only reason buyers talked to these reps at all is because of social connections, they did not think the reps contributed much to business. Customers of unreformed SOEs said that they were not going to shift any buying to these reps, but the reps' poor performance had little impact on purchase decisions because their company had fixed relationships with suppliers as mandated by the state industry administration.

(In other words, these SOEs were sometimes still operating under the state planning system) Sometimes, decisions were made by the top managers, based on connections, but not connections of the reps.

The Evolving Role of *Guanxi*

One of our key interests in this discussion has been to demonstrate that reform of sales management practices actually had practical impact on sales rep performance and customer buying behavior. Through a better recruiting process, the strongly reformed SOEs got better quality reps to start with. Through better training, the SOEs taught them more in the beginning, and supported continuous learning by reps beyond the initial training. Customers of strongly reformed SOEs were much happier with the sales reps they dealt with. They responded by placing trial orders, and eventually began shifting sales to SOEs with such professional reps.

Customers of SOEs which had failed to reform the sales force thought the reps were poor, and bought mainly because they still followed state planning, or engaged in traditional 'deal making' based on *guanxi* networks of the 'big boss'. Once the buying function in such companies begin to reform, and purchasing managers start making autonomous purchase decisions, they are very likely to shift suppliers, because professional reps are able to tailor offers and interactions to give customers greater value.

Guanxi played a role in both strongly reformed and unreformed SOEs, but it was a very different role, at different levels. The often-heard refrain "you can't sell anything in China without connections" is actually true in the very traditional sector, but professional sales reps can develop sales where they lack prior *guanxi*. This project showed that traditional *guanxi* was important among SOEs which had not yet begun any serious reform efforts. Reps in these unreformed SOEs believed that *guanxi* was the main reason customers bought, and viewed their jobs mainly as social interaction, with little product knowledge or consultative selling skill required. *Guanxi* was, in fact, important for sales. However, it was not actually the reps' own *guanxi* that mattered. Customers of these reps said that the reps had little influence on purchase decisions.

Rather, higher level *guanxi* was critical – top level connections between buyer, seller, and the state administration. Purchase decisions depended on state directives or deals made by high-level management. This is the traditional system behind the "you can't sell anything in China without connections" mantra. Generally, these are companies which have not engaged in much reform. Neither reps in the supplier SOE nor purchasing managers in the customer SOE had much decision authority. In the top-down traditional management style, low-level employees simply implement what the big boss directs.

However, among the strongly reforming SOEs, sales reps did not need prior *guanxi* to gain trial orders. Many customers (particularly among companies which were themselves reforming) were happy to deal with them. Purchasing managers appreciated the professionalism and knowledge of these reps, and *guanxi* was not a necessary prior condition. These customers were willing to let *guanxi* develop based on concurrent development of business relationships. It became important for building up a bigger volume business relationship, but the professional reps in the strong reform SOEs were skilled at building the traditional *guanxi* on top of the business relationship. Then they could use their newly developing *guanxi* to facilitate more information exchange, which helped them adapt to customers better. In other words, *guanxi* played an important role in developing the modern consultative sales approach of relationship marketing.

Figure 1: *Guanxi* in Traditional and Modern Sales

Modern professional managers set policy, but delegate responsibility. Reps must develop sales, and purchasing managers have real responsibility in procurement. The interests of both sides are well served with strong information exchange, but Asian societies traditionally value business secrecy. Thus, *guanxi* was not disappearing, but its role was shifting; in particular, it gives better access to information. Many companies in the Asian business environment are still quite secretive about information. Modern sales needs *guanxi* at the level of sales and purchasing, where it plays an important role in facilitating information flow needed for modern relationship marketing. Reps with *guanxi* have a better chance of using modern sales skills to fit their products to customer needs, as suggested in Speece (2001).

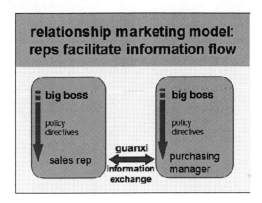

This shift in *guanxi* is summarized in Figure 1. In the traditional sales system, most of the *guanxi* is at the higher level. Deals are made between the 'big boss' of both the supplier and customer companies, based on guanxi at this top level. Sales reps and purchasing managers mainly implement specific directives from the big bosses. They do not really need much product knowledge or many selling skills in this system. In modern management, the 'big boss' mostly sets policy, and decision authority for day-to-day operations is delegated down to professional managers. Sales reps are responsible for generating sales, not simply processing orders.

When they are well educated, have strong product knowledge, and develop good sales skills, the traditional refrain that 'you can't sell anything in China without connections' is not true, according to Chinese SOE customers who had experience with competent reps. Customers were willing to place trial orders with reps they had not known before. They did expect that the *guanxi* connections would develop over time if the initial trial orders proved that the supplier, and the rep, could serve the customer well. This *guanxi* was between rep and decision influencers in the customer company, and its purpose was to facilitate information flow, so that the supplier could adapt to customers in ever increasing customization to their needs.

Conclusions

These findings and observations all indicate that China has made progress perhaps more rapidly and more widely than many observers realize. Modernization and professionalization of business operations may originally have come mainly because of foreign influence in coastal areas, but direct foreign influence does not seem to be necessary. Even a decade ago, the process was strong in the interior, away from any foreign influence, as well as the coastal areas. Some SOEs were upgrading their sales forces even where there were few foreigners around, little real competition from foreigners, and no foreign customers. Better sales forces clearly paid off for these SOEs. They often found it easier to get initial sales, customer satisfaction with the reps was higher, and customers started shifting sales to them away from companies with less professional sales forces.

Reps themselves were happy with the process and planned to stay, not simply using the strongly reformed SOEs as a training ground to gain experience so they could find another job. Thus, over time, the cumulative knowledge base about sales will grow and make the process sustainable. Many other SOEs will see this, and strengthen their own commitment to developing a strong sales force before they lose too much market share. The process can only gather momentum in the future.

Professionalization of sales in the strong reform SOEs is beginning to shift practice toward Western concepts of relationship marketing. This is not necessarily Westernization of sales; rather, Western concepts of relationship marketing are being adapted to the Chinese context, not adopted completely. Or, looking from the Chinese viewpoint, traditional Chinese practices are being modernized to fit the needs of modern business, as *guanxi* is integrated into relationship marketing, not discarded. In other words, cultures evolve. *Guanxi* seems to be a dynamic, rather than a static concept, changing as the economy changes, as the knowledge base in society grows, as other views come in from outside Chinese culture.

Where once *guanxi* may have been a necessary condition for any transaction to take place, it is no longer necessary. *Guanxi* is still useful, in particular, it gives better access to information, and thus is important for strengthening the foundations upon which relationship marketing is built. Given that many Asian companies are still secretive about information, reps with *guanxi* are better able to use modern sales skills to fit their products to customer needs. In the long run, this fusion of professional sales and traditional *guanxi* skills will make some Chinese companies very tough competitors in Asian markets.

References

Arias, J.T.G. 1998. A relationship marketing approach to guanxi. *European Journal of Marketing.* 32(1/2):145-156

Chen, C.C. & Chen, X.P. 2009. Negative externalities of close guanxi within organizations. *Asia Pacific Journal of Management.* 26(1):37-53

China Statistical Yearbook (CSY) 1997. Beijing: China Statistical Publishing

Gan, B. 1998. Two fundamental changes and SOE marketing and sales. *Business Economy & Management.* 2:41-43 [in Chinese]

Han, J. 1999. *Sales Force Management of Machinery State Owned Enterprises in Shaanxi, China.* Unpublished MBA thesis. Bangkok: Asian Institute of Technology

Harker, M.J. 1999. Relationship marketing defined? An examination of current relationship marketing definitions. *Marketing Intelligence & Planning.* 17(1):13-20

Lambert, D.M., Sharma, A., & Levy, M. 1997. What information can relationship marketers obtain from customer evaluations of salespeople. *Industrial Marketing Management.* 26:177-187

Luo, Y. 1997. Guanxi: principles, philosophies, and implications. *Human Systems Management.* 16:43-51

—. 2008. The changing Chinese culture and business behavior: The perspective of intertwinement between guanxi and corruption. *International Business Review.* 17(2):188-193

Shao, Z. 1998. Current Status of SOE Marketing and Sales and Counter Measures. *Journal of the Shanxi Economy and Finance University.* 3:31-33

Speece, M. 2001. Asian management style: An introduction. *Journal of Managerial Psychology.* 16(2):86-96

Srijumpa, R., Larpsiri, R. & Speece, M. 2004. Qualitative exploratory research on customer acceptance of technology in financial services. In R.D.Sharma & H.Chahal (Eds.). *Research Methodology in Commerce and Management.* New Delhi: Anmol. 60-86

Tsang, E.W.K. 1998. Can guanxi be a source of sustained competitive advantage for doing business in China? *Academy of Management Executive.* 12(2):64-73

Wang, W. 1998a. Analysis of Chinese enterprises' marketing and sales: Status and suggestions. *Business Research.* 1:36-37 [in Chinese]

—. 1998b. On Focused Marketing and Sales Management. *Theory and Practice in Economics and Finance.* 3:93-94 [in Chinese]

Weitz, B.A. & Bradford, K.D. 1999. Personal selling and sales management: A relationship marketing perspective. *Journal of the Academy of Marketing Science.* 27(2):241-254

Wong, Y.H. & Chan, R.Y.K. 1999. Relationship Marketing in China: Guanxi, favouritism and adaptation. *Journal of Business Ethics.* 22:107-118

Wu, X. & Speece, M. 1998. Sales force development in China. *Journal of International Selling and Sales Management.* 4(1):3-19

Xu, N. & Cai, Y. 1998. Market-orientation: Necessity for modern enterprises. *Shanghai Enterprises.* 2:29-32 [in Chinese]

Zhang, S. & Xie, R. 1992. The marketing and selling issues in the market socialism economy. *Exploring* (Chong Qing). June:110-112 [in Chinese]

Zhuang, G., Xi, Y. & Tsang, A.S.L. 2010. Power, conflict, and cooperation: The impact of guanxi in Chinese marketing channels. *Industrial Marketing Management.* 39:137–149

CHAPTER SIX

ETHICAL ATTITUDES IN BUSINESS:
A COMPARATIVE STUDY IN SEVEN COUNTRIES

CHRIS PERRYER, GEOFFREY N. SOUTAR
AND CATHERINE JORDAN

Abstract

This paper reports the results of an exploratory study which investigated the similarity in attitudes to a range of business ethical questions in seven countries. Data were obtained from respondents in Australia, Singapore, Indonesia, China, the Philippines, the USA and the UK. Analysis of the data using discriminant analysis revealed two functions. The first related to self-advancement at the expense of a co-worker, and the second to misuse of organisational assets. On the first function, China, Singapore, UK, Australia and the US were relatively close, while Indonesia and particularly the Philippines were distinctly different. On the second function, the Philippines differed considerably when compared with the other cultural groupings.

Introduction

Current ethical theory provides managers with a range of models that their proponents argue are useful in understanding ethical dilemmas or predicting ethical behaviour. However, because values and ethical norms vary from place to place, it is often difficult for managers to determine how best to apply that theory. In addition, managers are often constrained by home country legislation from implementing practices that are acceptable or even expected in different cultural settings in which they may be operating. A considerable body of research has examined differences between ethical norms across a range of different cultures. However, it may be more useful to practitioners and academics to investigate similarities in ethical norms. Understanding similarities will provide managers with a better understanding of what is likely to be ethically acceptable across cultures, rather than simply knowing what is likely to be unacceptable. Having such an understanding will enable managers to identify transcultural ethical norms that assist in predicting behaviour, as well as developing codes of practice that are congruent with employee values across cultures.

Literature Review

Business ethics has become an issue of considerable concern for organisations around the world, largely because of recent well publicised corporate collapses and scandals. Companies have responded with training seminars and codes of conduct, while educators have introduced new ethics courses or strengthened existing ones and researchers have attempted to develop a body of theory that can help to explain managers' ethical behaviour.

There is, however, an argument that ethics theory has not been particularly helpful to the international manager. Existing theory may be appropriate in principle, but it is difficult to apply practically. For example, one widely accepted theory is ethical relativism, which is based on the idea that the "rightness" of an activity can be different in different cultural settings. The opposing theory, absolutism, suggests the rightness of an activity is universal. Ethical relativism theory would suggest that, when managers are transferred to a new cultural setting, they can adapt to local conditions, but this is not simple in practice. Managers are often constrained by home country legislation and practice from implementing practices that are acceptable, or even expected, in a different cultural setting. This situation becomes even more complicated when a number of different cultures are involved in an international venture. Indeed, it has been argued that new theory needs to be developed that will guide international managers in addressing ethical dilemmas (Velazquez 2000).

Many researchers have examined the influence cultural values have on attitudes to ethics, building on the extensive body of literature attesting to cultural differences (Hofstede 1980; Hofstede 1983; Hofstede 1993; Hofstede 2002). Recent studies that have examined the influence of culture have generally found it to be a significant predictor of ethical behaviour or attitudes (Erdener 1996; Jackson & Artola 1997; Nyaw & Ng 1994; Perryer & Jordan 2002; Phau & Kea 2007; Robertson et al. 2002; Singhapakdi et al. 2001), although Cortese (1989) and Kracher, Chatterjee and Lundquist (2002) found the impact of ethnic-cultural background was inconclusive.

Another limitation for practitioners with much of the previous research is that it is based on samples of convenience, and often only compares two or perhaps three countries. For example, Beekun et al. (2005) compared ethical perceptions in the US and Russia, Kracher et al. (2002) India and the US, Perryer and Jordan (2002) in Australia and Singapore, and Preim and Shaffer (2001) in the US, Portugal and Hong Kong. Studies involving five or more countries are more difficult to find; although Jackson (1997) (five countries) and Jackson and Artola (1997) (six countries) are two exceptions. Managers who operate in a particular geographic region have not been well served by prior research. Studies that include a greater number of countries are likely to be of more practical value to such managers.

The second important limitation of many previous studies is that they identify differences between cultures and sometimes discuss why such differences may exist. Of more use to practitioners would be studies that focus on ethical values or norms that are similar in a number of cultures. The third important limitation for practitioners in the Asian region is that very few studies have obtained data from countries other than Japan, China and Singapore. This is of particular concern to managers of companies whose employees may regularly move between predominantly Muslim countries, such as Indonesia, predominantly Catholic countries, such as the Philippines, and predominantly Buddhist or Confucian cultures in much of the rest of Asia. The present study, which is discussed in the next section, was undertaken with respondents aligned to a number of countries to overcome these issues.

The Present Study

The data examined in this paper were collected as part of a larger study, in which respondents were asked to nominate the country to which their cultural and ethical attitudes were most closely aligned. Respondents indicating cultural alignment with the countries of interest formed the sample for the study (n=356). In order to ensure comparability across the sub-samples, only respondents with tertiary education qualifications were included in the analysis. Graduate students made up 74 percent of the sample, bachelor degree graduates 3 percent and undergraduates 23 percent. The sample contained 54 percent males and 46 percent females. Respondents were asked to indicate their age group based on five year increments. The median age was in the 31 to 35 age group and the modal age was in the 26 to 30 age group. Responses indicated cultural and ethical alignment with Australia (n=65), Singapore (n=61), Indonesia (n=41),

China (n=33), the Philippines (n=64), the United States of America (n=46) and the United Kingdom (n=46).

Fourteen items based on the seventeen item scale developed by Newstrom and Ruch (1975), and three items taken from Peterson et al. (2001) were used to measure respondents' ethical perceptions. These items have been widely used in business ethics research (Akaah & Lund 1994; Jackson & Artola 1997; Kantor & Weisberg 2002; Perryer 2005; Perryer & Jordan 2002). Participants were also asked to indicate the extent to which they felt it was acceptable to engage in a range of behaviours, such as using office supplies for personal use, or claiming credit for a colleague's work. Responses were obtained on a five-point Likert-type scale, ranging from 1 (strongly agree) to 5 (strongly disagree), such that higher values indicates 'higher' ethical standards. As missing data were minimal, amounting to less than 1 percent in total, such values were imputed using the Expectation-Maximization (EM) method, which enabled the total data set to be analysed.

As a first step descriptive statistics were calculated. Relationships in the data were then analysed using discriminant analysis with SPSS version 19. Discriminant analysis is a multivariate analysis technique that differentiates groups on one or more dimensions where the dependent variable is non-metric or categorical (in this case nominal) and the independent variables are metric or numerical (in this case interval). Country of cultural alignment was used as the dependent variable and individual questionnaire items were used as the independent variables in this case.

Results

Means and standard deviations were computed for each item across the seven groups and in total; these are shown in the Appendix. Numerical differences in the means and standard deviations suggested there was a degree of variation in the groups' ethical perceptions. When considering the total scores for the items, some items clearly demonstrated general agreement between countries, as shown by the small variation (low standard deviation). These items included "use company email and computing facilities for personal use", "conceal own errors", take extra breaks at work" and "ignore other people's violations of company policies". The means for these items range from 2.68 to 3.33, suggesting a "neither agree nor disagree" response. The total scores for other items showed high variation (large standard deviations) across the cultural groups, including "use the company phone for local personal calls on company time", "pass the blame for your own errors to another co-worker", and "claim credit for someone else's work". When the means for the latter two items were considered (4.01 and 3.90 respectively), it seems respondents tended toward the 'disagree' to 'strongly disagree' responses for these items. Of particular interest is the generally lower mean response of the Philippines group, a fact which was clearly evident in the discriminant analysis. The standard deviations for each cultural group on each item have also been reported in the Appendix. These provide information about the level of agreement of respondents within each cultural group. These are all similar across the groups for each item. This is important, and one of the assumptions of discriminant analysis.

An initial analysis of the data revealed that one item ("It is okay to imply that you are a potential customer to obtain information about a competitor's products or services") showed no significant differences across the seven groups (a non-significant F statistic in the equivalent of a one way ANOVA). Consequently, this item was removed from the analysis. This was consistent with the descriptive statistics that showed the means across the seven groups were similar. After removing this item and re-running the discriminant analysis, the remaining items were significant across the groups as the F statistics between the groups ranged from 2.90 to 119.54, all of which were significant well beyond the 1 percent level.

The discriminant analysis revealed two significant functions within the data. Using the I^2 statistic (Peterson & Mahajan 1976) as a guide, the two functions explained 38% of the group differences, which suggested there were real differences in the groups' ethical perceptions. One of the advantages of discriminant analysis is that these relationships can be displayed diagrammatically using the structural correlations between the functions and the predictor variables to describe the estimated functions and the groups' centroids to understand group differences (Soutar & Clarke 1981).The map displaying the relationships between the groups and functions is shown in Figure 1. For clarity and ease of interpretation, items that had structural correlations that were less than 0.40 are not shown (Hair et al. 2010). As is accepted practice, the structural correlations are presented as vectors, with the direction of the vector showing the nature of the relationship (positive or negative) and the length of the vector showing the strength of the relationship (Johnson 1977). The cultural groups are located on the map using their group centroid values, which are also shown on Figure 1.

Figure 1: The Relationships between Cultural Groupings and Ethical Perceptions

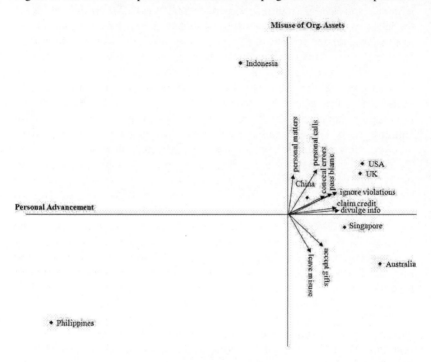

Discussion

The present study examined the group differences and similarities between seven cultural groups' ethical perceptions. The results obtained revealed that all of the groups differed significantly in terms of their ethical perceptions. Descriptive statistics suggested the variation across the responses for some items was small and that the means tended towards a neutral response. For these items it seems there was general agreement of neutrality in relation to the ethical perceptions for these items across the seven cultural groups. Other items were notable for their large standard deviations across the groups. This large variation implied general disagreement across the cultural groups in terms of their ethical perceptions of these items.

The discriminant analysis identified two functions. The first related to behaviours such as concealing personal errors, divulging confidential information and claiming credit for others' work. These items were categorised as *personal advancement at the expense of co-workers*. On the first function, China, Singapore, UK, Australia and the USA were relatively close, while Indonesia and, particularly, the Philippines were distinctly different. The finding that the group centroid values for the UK, Australia and the USA were close was expected, given the cultural, economic and historical similarities of these countries. Singapore is also a developed, first world country that has inherited its legal and commercial norms from the UK and has close trading links with Australia and the USA. Consequently, despite its Confucian influence, its location on the map was not unexpected. The finding that China is much closer to these countries than it is to the other developing countries in this study is of particular interest and less easy to explain. It may be that China's rapid development to being a world power, along with its involvement in international bodies such as the World Trade Organisation, has led to convergence with the ethical attitudes of people in business in the developed world. More likely, however, is that the finding is an artefact of the sample, which included only tertiary educated people, who may not be representative of the population as a whole. The finding though, is of theoretical and practical significance, as business people from the west might expect ethical attitudes of tertiary educated Chinese people to mirror their own attitudes in many ways, at least in respect of the two functions identified in this study, while this may not be true of non–tertiary educated Chinese people. The findings in respect of Indonesia and, particularly, the Philippines are more difficult to explain. The centroid values of these two countries suggest they are different from their Asian neighbours in their attitudes towards advancing their personal situation at the expense of others. This may be due to the fact that these countries are less egalitarian that the other countries in this study, resulting in a "personal advancement at any cost" attitude among tertiary educated people. Further research that investigates the antecedents of these attitudes is likely to increase our understanding of these issues.

The second function related to behaviours such as doing personal business during work time and the misuse of leave entitlements. These items were categorised as the *misuse of organisational assets*. On this function the USA, the UK, China and Singapore were closely grouped, with Australia having a more "relaxed" attitude to the misuse of organisational assets, followed at a greater distance by the Philippines. The surprising finding was the value for Indonesia, which was considerably higher than the other countries. As with the first function, it is difficult to suggest reasons why this might be so, and further research is clearly needed to understand the antecedents of the findings.

Some limitations of this study should be noted. Firstly, since this is an exploratory study, the interpretation and labelling of each of the functions should be considered tentative. Further research is needed to confirm the results of this study, and to extend our understanding of ethical attitudes in business. Secondly, the use of self-reports, although common in social science research (Chang et al. 2010; Podsakoff & Organ 1986), can increase the possibility of common method bias (Doty & Glick 1998). Thirdly, the study did not attempt to control for potential social desirability response effects. This was done in order to ensure a parsimonious questionnaire. It is acknowledged however, that such effects have the potential to impact on responses in ethics research (Fernandes & Randall 1992). Fourthly, the study did not consider the reasons why differences exist, reducing the explanatory value of the findings. Further work is needed to identify the antecedents to ethical attitudes of business people in the cultural groups examined. It may be that variables such as personality, situational variables and moral intensity can explain some of the variance in ethical attitudes, but this study did not seek to examine those variables, and future research that investigates these variables would be useful.

Conclusions

This exploratory study used a data analysis technique, often under-utilised in management research, to investigate similarities and differences in ethical attitudes in seven cultural groups, some of which have received limited attention in the literature, but which are of growing regional and international importance. A number of insights into ethical attitudes emerged from the study, but the findings are descriptive rather than explanatory. The analytic technique used in the study is useful in describing what those attitudes are, but it does not offer possible explanations for those attitudes. Further research is needed to confirm these findings and to investigate potential antecedents to people's ethical attitudes.

References

Akaah, I.P. & Lund, D. 1994. The influence of personal and organizational values on marketing professionals' ethical behaviour. *Journal of Business Ethics*. 13:417-430

Beekun, R.I., Westerman, J. & Barghouti, J. 2005. Utility of ethical frameworks in determining behavioral intention: A comparison of the U.S. and Russia. *Journal of Business Ethics*. 61:235-247

Cortese, A.J. 1989. The interpersonal approach to morality: A gender and cultural analysis. *Journal of Social Psychology.* 129(4):429-441

Erdener, C.B. 1996. Ethnicity, nationality and gender: A cross-cultural comparison of business ethical decisions in four countries. *International Journal of Human Resource Management.* 7(4):866-877

Hofstede, G. 1980. Motivation, leadership, and organization: do American theories apply abroad? *Organizational Dynamics.* 9(1):42

—. 1983.,'The cultural relativity of organizational practices and theories. *Journal of International Business Studies.* 14(2):75-90

—. 1993. Cultural constraints in management theories. *Academy of Management Executive.* 7(1):81-84

—. 2002. *A Summary of My Ideas about National Culture Differences.* Retrieved May 30, 2002 from http://cwis.kub.nl

Jackson, T. 1997. Management ethics and corporate policy: A cross-cultural comparison. *Journal of Management Studies.* 37(3):349-369

Jackson, T. & Artola, M.C. 1997. Ethical beliefs and management behavior: A cross cultural comparison. *Journal of Business Ethics.* 16(11):1163-1173

Kantor, J. & Weisberg, J. 2002. Ethical attitudes and ethical behavior: Are managers role models? *International Journal of Manpower.* 23(8):687-703

Kracher, B., Chatterjee, A. & Lundquist, A.R. 2002. Factors related to the cognitive moral development of business students and business professionals in India and the United States: Nationality, education, sex and gender. *Journal of Business Ethics.* 35:255-268

Newstrom, J.W. & Ruch, W.A. 1975. The ethics of management and the management of ethics. *MSU Business Topics.* Winter:29-37

Nyaw, M.-K. & Ng, I. 1994. A comparative analysis of ethical beliefs: A four country study. *Journal of Business Ethics.* 13(7):543-555

Perryer, C. 2005. Towards a factor structure of perceptions of ethical behaviour. *Australian and New Zealand Academy of Management.* Canberra, Australia. 12

Perryer, C. & Jordan, C. 2002. The influence of gender, age, culture and other factors on ethical beliefs: A comparative study in Australia and Singapore. *Public Administration and Management: An Interactive Journal.* 7(4):367-382

Peterson, D., Rhoads, A. & Vaught, B.C. 2001. Ethical beliefs of business professionals: A study of gender, age and external factors. *Journal of Business Ethics.* 31:225-232

Phau, I. & Kea, G. 2007. Attitudes of universtiy students towards business ethics: A cross-national investigation of Australia, Singapore and Hong Kong. *Journal of Business Ethics.* 72:61-75

Preim, R.L. & Shaffer, M. 2001. Resolving moral dilemmas in business: A multicountry study. *Business and Society.* 40(2):197-219

Robertson, C.J., Crittenden, W.F., Brady, M.K. & Hoffman, J.J. 2002. Situational ethics across borders: A multicultural examination. *Journal of Business Ethics.* 38:327-338

Singhapakdi, A., Karande, K., Rao, C.P. & Vitell, S.J. 2001. How important are ethics and social responsibility? - A multinational study of marketing professionals. *European Journal of Marketing.* 35(1/2):133-155

Velazquez, M. 2000. Globalization and the failure of ethics. *Business Ethics Quarterly.* 10(1):343-352

Appendix: Descriptive Statistics for Cultural Groups' Ethical Perceptions

Item "It is okay to ..."	Australia M (SD)	Singapore M (SD)	Indonesia M (SD)	China M (SD)	Philippines M (SD)	USA M (SD)	UK M (SD)	Total M (SD)
use company office supplies for personal use	3.22 (1.04)	3.20 (.95)	3.15 (.96)	3.55 (1.18)	1.95(.82)	3.35 (1.18)	3.22 (1.19)	3.03 (1.15)
use the company phone for local personal calls on company time	2.69 (1.06)	2.57 (.92)	3.10 (1.00)	3.41 (1.24)	2.30 (.85)	3.02 (1.18)	2.93 (1.20)	2.79 (1.09)
use company email and computing facilities for personal use	2.57 (.98)	2.61 (.84)	2.37 (.66)	3.09 (1.06)	2.56 (.94)	2.98 (1.14)	2.80 (1.00)	2.68 (.97)
attend to personal matters in company time	2.75 (1.05)	3.34 (.95)	3.59 (.97)	3.44 (.84)	2.45 (.99)	3.70 (.87)	3.41 (.83)	3.17 (1.04)
to use the company phone for long distance personal phone calls	3.88 (1.04)	4.39 (.67)	4.24 (.80)	4.12 (1.08)	1.78 (1.02)	4.20 (.75)	4.13 (.81)	3.73 (1.28)
use specific purpose company leave entitlements (such as sick leave) for other personal purposes	3.88 (.99)	3.80 (.96)	2.39 (.70)	3.42 (.90)	2.42 (.94)	3.00 (1.32)	2.87 (1.28)	3.15 (1.18)
recruit personnel from competing businesses on competing company's time or property	3.05 (1.15)	3.16 (1.08)	2.68 (1.01)	2.94 (1.20)	2.53 (.94)	3.76 (1.10)	3.13 (1.24)	3.03 (1.15)
incorporate a mini-vacation with a company-paid trip at company expense	3.43 (1.12)	3.21 (.97)	3.07 (1.10)	3.56 (1.22)	2.17 (.98)	3.24 (1.14)	3.17 (1.23)	3.08 (1.18)
imply that you are a potential customer to obtain information about a competitor's products or services	2.95 (1.12)	2.56 (.92)	2.78 (.85)	2.94 (.86)	2.75 (.87)	2.76 (1.30)	2.70 (1.11)	2.77 (1.02)

Item "It is okay to ..."	Australia	Singapore	Indonesia	China	Philippines	USA	UK	Total
	M (SD)	M (SD)	M (SD)	M (SD)	M (SD)	M (SD)	M (SD)	M (SD)
accept gifts and favors in exchange for preferential treatment	3.85 (.78)	4.11 (.95)	2.51 (.75)	3.78 (.66)	2.34 (.98)	3.78 (.47)	3.78 (.47)	3.45 (1.03)
pass the blame for your own errors to another co-worker	4.65 (.74)	4.66 (.51)	3.93 (1.08)	4.53 (.98)	1.66 (1.04)	4.67 (.47)	4.59 (.50)	4.01 (1.37)
divulge confidential company information to outsiders	4.75 (.47)	4.67 (.47)	3.76 (.83)	4.53 (.98)	2.28 (1.00)	4.76 (.43)	4.74 (.44)	4.16 (1.16)
give gifts and favors in exchange for preferential treatment	3.72 (.89)	3.74 (1.12)	2.34 (.62)	3.44 (.72)	2.16 (.96)	3.78 (.47)	3.39 (.54)	3.22 (1.05)
claim credit for someone else's work	4.60 (.81)	4.46 (.56)	3.44 (1.23)	4.09 (.89)	1.64 (1.09)	4.83 (.57)	4.67 (.73)	3.90 (1.42)
conceal your own errors	3.80 (.78)	3.44 (.94)	3.22 (.76)	3.44 (.72)	2.02 (.95)	3.91 (.28)	3.83 (.38)	3.33 (1.00)
take extra breaks at work	3.43 (1.00)	3.00 (.91)	2.61 (.70)	3.00 (.57)	2.88 (1.13)	3.09 (.55)	3.02 (.58)	3.03 (.88)
ignore other people's violations of company policies	3.88 (.57)	3.39 (.69)	3.22 (.69)	3.25 (.67)	1.75 (.76)	3.98 (.33)	3.93 (.33)	3.30 (.99)

Note: M = mean, SD = standard deviation.

CHAPTER SEVEN

BUSINESS CONSTRAINTS AND RECESSIONARY EFFECTS ON SMALL FIRMS IN VIETNAM: A CASE STUDY OF THE RETAIL CLOTHING INDUSTRY

VICTOR EGAN

Abstract

Small firms have long been touted as a driving force for economic development by way of entrepreneurial innovation, and the employment opportunities created. In this context, the efficiency of the small firm sector should be of paramount concern to governments, particularly those with the responsibility of delivering economic growth and improved living conditions to the citizens of less developed countries. This paper presents the results of a study which sought to explore the short-term impact of the 2008 global economic recession, as well as the longer-term business constraints that impact on the efficiency and potential for growth for small firms in Vietnam. To this end, the study focused on the retail clothing industry as a basic barometer of the health of the Vietnamese economy. The results of the study suggest that the global economic recession produced a decline in sales of 20-50 percent (average 32 percent) over the same period the previous year. The results further indicate that a number of constraints to the performance of small firms were common. These include strong competition, government taxes, poor infrastructure, and lack of skills of both employees and owners.

Introduction

The development of a vibrant and efficient private business sector is of critical importance in the quest to deliver sustainable economic growth and rising living standards to any society (Ramachandran & Shah 1999). In support of an efficient private sector, there are many factors that influence sustained economic growth, including geography, education, access to land and finance, and infrastructure (Bleaney & Nishiyama 2002). In addition, entrepreneurial activity and effective small business has often been proffered as an important mechanism to promote employment, productivity, and innovation, and hence, progress economic development (Daniels & Mead 1998; Klapper & Delgado 2007; Spencer & Gomez 2004; van Praag & Versloot 2007). As such, most governments recognise the significance of the small business sector, and consequently, place great emphasis on promoting this sector of the economy (Daniels & Mead 1998). In the case of Vietnam, small firms generate 53 percent of gross domestic product (GDP), and account for 70 percent of total employment and 90 percent of new job creation (Small and medium enterprises' week to launch in Hanoi 2008).

However, constraints to small firms often impact on their efficiency, and potential for growth. These constraints include unfair competition from the informal sector, poor infrastructure, lack of access to finance, low productivity of human resources, inequality in tax administration, and corruption (Kellow 2007; UNCTAD 2006; UNCTAD 2007; World Bank 1993). In addition to the longer-term business constraints, the world entered a period of global economic recession in 2008. While the effects of the recession on large economies have featured prominently in the media and academic writing, less developed countries have also been heavily impacted as collateral damage from reduced export markets.

This paper will explore two issues involving small firms in Vietnam. Firstly, the immediate impact of the 2008 global economic recession; and secondly, the longer-term business constraints that impose limitations on both efficient operation, and potential for future growth. The paper will begin by briefly reviewing the background to the global economic recession, as well as the effect of the recession on Vietnam. The nature of small firms in Vietnam will then be outlined, before presenting the methodology, results, and a discussion of the findings.

The 2008 Global Economic Recession

Following a period of economic boom, a global financial crisis was precipitated in late-2007 by a collapse of the securitised US sub-prime mortgage market (Loftus 2008). The epicentre was on Wall Street, and was driven by the rampant greed of financiers and inadequate government regulation (Gould 2008; Krugman 2008). This event had a global ripple effect, which subsequently resulted in falling world stock markets, the collapse of financial institutions, a plethora of government rescue packages to bail out distressed financial systems, and widespread economic recession (Shah 2009). During 2008, the global economic recession impacted heavily on country institutions and economies; 58 banks collapsed or merged, bank write-downs reached US$2.8trillion, and imports/exports worldwide declined rapidly (IMF 2009; OECD 2009).

Effects of the Global Economic Recession on Vietnam

Given the connectedness of world economies, Vietnam could not remain isolated from the global economic recession (Lombra 2009; Nguyen 2009). Consequently, Vietnam's gross domestic product (GDP) growth rate declined from 8.5 percent in 2007 to 6.2 percent in 2008. Likewise, exports fell by 24.5 percent, due mainly to shrinking demands in the US, Europe, and Japan (Pincus 2009; Vietnam: An On-The-Ground Perspective 2009). Furthermore, tightening global credit reduced the inflows of foreign direct investment (FDI) to Vietnam. For instance, FDI in the first quarter of 2009 was only 30 percent of the FDI for the same period in 2008. In addition, domestic consumption declined as a result of job cuts and wage reduction. There were 500,000 job losses in 2008, leading to an unemployment rate of 5.6 percent (Vietnam: An On-The-Ground Perspective 2009, 2).

Small Firms in Vietnam

Prior to 1986, the Vietnamese economy had suffered grievously from institutional weaknesses, and isolation from global trade. Most government financial support was provided to large state-owned enterprises (SOEs), which were highly inefficient in their operation (Farrell and Downing 1997). To revive the parlous state of the economy, the Vietnamese government introduced a reform programme known as *Doi Moi* ('open system') in 1986. The open policy abolished central planning, and enabled increased exports and inflows of FDI (Mansurel and Smit 2000). The government also started to support non-SOE sectors, especially privately-owned small firms (Phan 2008a, 2008b).

By 2007, Vietnam had 332,500 privately-owned small firms, and the number was growing at an annual rate of 20 percent (Tran et al. 2008). The vast majority of Vietnamese small firms are family-based (Meyer, Tran and Nguyen 2006; Pham 2009). Significant proportions of the total number of small firms are located in the main commercial centres of Ho Chi Minh City (HCMC) (25 percent) and Hanoi (15 percent), while no other city has more than 4 percent (Tran et al. 2008; Asian Development

Bank 2009b). As is the case in any country, Vietnamese small firms are an important factor in the growth of the country's economy. These firms generate 53 percent of GDP, and account for 70 percent of total employment and 90 percent of new job creation (Small and medium enterprises' week to launch in Hanoi 2008).

As a consequence of the global economic recession, 7,000 small firms were dissolved, and another 3,000 ceased operation in 2008 (Phuoc 2009). According to research conducted in late-2008, 80 percent of small firms had financial problems, having suffered substantial decline in income (Many SMEs will go into bankruptcy 2009). Since nearly 90 percent of the output generated by small firms in Vietnam serves the domestic market, the direct impact of the economic recession was more likely through weak domestic demand and higher unemployment, rather than a decline in exports (Asian Development Bank 2009a).

Business Constraints on Small Firms in Vietnam

While the global economic recession provided a short-term challenge for small firms in Vietnam, there are also longer-term business constraints that compound the recessionary effects, and affect efficient operation and potential for growth. The major constraints on business in Vietnam are identified next.

Limited accessed to finance

Small firms in Vietnam have historically faced credit constraints for three reasons (Farrell and Downing 1997; Kokko and Sjoholm 2006; Rand 2007; Thomsen 2007). Firstly, there is substantial requirement of collateral for the granting of credit. For example, banks often require collateral worth 100-300 percent of the value of the loan. Secondly, bank loan procedures are complicated, costly, and time consuming. Thirdly, poor quality business plans from uneducated borrowers discourage banks from lending. Consequently, less than 7 percent of small firms in Vietnam use bank credit to start up or finance their businesses (Asian Development Bank 2009b).

Complex and time consuming registration procedures

A plethora of regulations and overlapping procedures make registration for business start-up in Vietnam very time consuming (Karkoviata 2001). It may take 50 days to go through 11 procedures before receiving approval for starting a business; this compares to the world average of 43 days, and only 3 days and 2 procedures in Canada (Ngo 2006). The reason for such inefficiency is the complex administrative system, lack of consistency in legal documents, and often intentional obstruction to provide opportunity for corrupt payments (Costs of doing business in Vietnam ranks no.1in the region 2008; http://www.heritage.org/Index/country.cfm?id=Vietnam).

High operating costs

Regardless of Vietnam's cheap labour cost, other operating costs are often much higher than in other Asian countries (UPS Snapshot for Small Businesses: Doing business in Vietnam 2008). These costs include property rent, and costs of electricity, telecommunications, and logistics. For example, in HCMC, the rental cost of a 32-40 square metre shop in a recognised commercial area is perhaps US$4,000 per month (High operating expenses limit capablilities to attract investment 2005).

Inflation

Inflation is normally high, averaging 7.7 percent between 2004 and 2006. In September 2008, it reached 28 percent. High inflation is detrimental to business for two reasons. Firstly, it weakens domestic demand; and secondly, it results in higher priced raw materials. Consequently, small firms suffer from both lower sale volumes, and higher operating costs. Furthermore, higher interest rates (usually associated with higher inflation) hinder the ability of small firms to access bank finance (Pincus 2009, 12-14; Solving problems facing Vietnamese SMEs 2008).

Lack of skills and education

Workers employed by small firms are predominantly unskilled and lowly educated (Kokko and Sjoholm 2006; VBF 2007), resulting in low productivity and increased labour costs (Vietnam economy: Education is a major concern 2009). A 2008 World Bank survey found that the quality of the Vietnamese workforce ranked 11th in a total of 12 Asian countries. Vietnam's labour productivity was evaluated lower than Indonesia, Thailand, and the Philippines, and overall, ranked Vietnam 77th among 125 nations globally (Denney 2008). In addition, most owners of small firms are hamstrung by poor management skills, little knowledge of new technology, and failure to apply effective human resource management practices (Hiemstra et al. 2006; King-Kauanui et al. 2006; Mansurel and Smit 2000; Nguyen 2007; Nguyen and Bryant 2004; SMEs vital for economy, but short of cash 2009).

Poor infrastructure

Despite the Government's efforts to improve the country's infrastructure, most small firms view the current infrastructure as inadequate, arguing that narrow and deteriorated roads cause traffic jams that delay the delivery of products and raw materials. In addition, power and water outages are common, greatly affecting productivity (Meyer et al. 2006; VBF 2007).

Government Intervention for Small Firms in Vietnam

Recognising the importance of small firms to the national economy and the constraints they face, the Vietnamese Government made a commitment from the early-2000s to support small firms by reforming the financial system (Hiemstra et al. 2006; Kokko and Sjoholm 2006). The Government issued Decrees in 2001, 2004, and 2006 in support of small business. These Decrees led to the establishment of the *SME Development Fund*, *Credit Guarantee Fund*, the *Human Resource Training Support Program 2004-2008*, and the *Five-Year SMEs Development Plan 2006-2010*. These initiatives were aimed at enhancing the competitiveness of small firms by improving the knowledge of both owners and employees, creating a more conductive business environment, and encouraging technology transfers among enterprises of different size (Tran et.al. 2008). The Government's major agency of SME support is the *Agency of Small and Medium Enterprises Development (ASMED)*. This agency is charged with helping the Government develop policies to support small firms development, organising training courses, and advising and facilitating access to new technology and equipment (Tran et.al. 2008)

To assist small firms cope with the impact of the 2008 global economic recession, the Government initiated tax and interest rate cuts, and established special credit funds for small firms. The Government also lengthened the payback period for both old and new loans. In addition to increasing the amount of credit available, the Government also implemented various capital mobilisation programs to boost domestic consumption (Hong 2009). These programs included tax reductions, subsidies for loan interest, increase in public investment, social security support, and a number of economic stimulus packages (Central bank, economists discuss interest rate subsidies 2009; Vietnam coping with global recession "reasonably well" - ADB economist 2009).

In 2009, the Vietnamese government issued a new decree in support of small firms. Specifically, newly established businesses may operate tax free for 2-4 years, as of the first profitable fiscal year, and will receive 50 percent tax reduction for the next 4-9 years. Furthermore, the government has encouraged financial institutions to establish credit guarantee funds for small firms, and provide supportive services such as financial counseling and investment management. Importantly, the Prime Minister also emphasised the need to establish plans to assist in the education of human resources, especially focusing on business administration (Decree about developing SMEs 2009).

In order to address the poor infrastructure, the Vietnamese government has tried to attract and encourage both domestic and foreign investment in the upgrade of transportation infrastructure by issuing tax incentive policies and ensuring the legal interests of the investors (Transportation Infrastructure Development in Vietnam 2009). The government has also been working towards addressing the complexity of business registration. Since late-2008, prospective business owners have been able to register their applications via the internet, which has reportedly reduced the registration period to 14 days (Nguyen 2008).

The Retail Clothing Industry in Vietnam

Vietnam's retail clothing industry is embedded within the global economic recession, business constraints, and government initiatives as described in the previous sections of this paper. This section now describes the specific characteristics of the retail clothing industry.

The retail clothing industry had been growing at an average rate of 15 percent per year during the period 2000-2007. In 2007, clothing sales accounted for 16.5 percent of total retail sales. The sales were derived through two forms of retail outlets; 'traditional' and 'modern'. 'Traditional' retailers include formal-sector privately-owned retail clothing shops located in markets or with street frontage, as well as informal-sector street vendors. On the other hand, 'modern' retailers are those who operate through large department stores. Traditional retailers account for about 80 percent of all clothing sales (Vietnam Retail Analysis (2008-2012) 2008).

Most traditional clothing retailers sell Chinese-made clothes (Discount garments fail to find buyers 2008). In 2007, 40-60 percent of sales was generated from Chinese clothes, while sales of domestic clothes accounted for only 25 percent (Vietnam loses clothing-market share 2008). Vietnamese consumers appear to prefer Chinese clothes because of the vibrant colours, superior design, and cheaper prices. A shirt made in China may cost only US$1.8-2.5, while a Vietnamese-made shirt may cost at least US$6. Street vendors often sell second-hand clothes coming from China. These clothes are extremely cheap (about US$0.5-0.6 per item), and their consumption is high in rural areas (Vietnam Retail Analysis (2008-2012) 2008). Competition is intense. Clothing retailers normally sell very similar products, and locate themselves very near to each other, or even next door (Vietnamese retailers brace themselves for the inevitable 2008).

The fashion industry is often perceived as a very profitable business sector, especially as living standards rise and disposable income increases. According to the Business Studies and Assistance Center (BSAC), 70 percent of urban Vietnamese consumers buy fashion products each month, and their spending for those items accounts for 18 percent of total monthly expenditure (Domestic fashion: weaknesses in distribution and designing stage 2008). Such strong consumer demand has exacerbated competition with strong growth in the number of small firms involved in the retail clothing industry (Vietnam retail analysis (2008-2012) 2008).

Methodology

The retail trade industry, in general, and the retail clothing industry more specifically, is usually considered a good barometer for the prevalent economic conditions in a country (Wickham 2009). This is especially the case in Vietnam where expenditure on clothing is high (Domestic fashion: weaknesses in distribution and designing stage 2008). Consequently, the retail clothing industry was purposely selected as the focus for the present study in order to gain an insight into business constraints, and the impact of the global economic recession on the Vietnamese economy.

While there is no universally accepted definition of a small firm (Burns 2007), the most commonly used metric is the number of employees (Harvie and Lee 2002). As such, a 'small enterprise' has been defined as one that employs <20 people (Harvie and Lee 2002). There is often a distinction made between service and manufacturing firms; for example, in Australia, small service firms are defined as those employing <20 people, while small manufacturing firms are those employing <100 (Harvie and Lee 2002). For the present study involving the retail clothing industry (i.e., services), 'small firm' was defined as one employing <20 workers.

The sample for the study consisted of 30 'traditional' retail clothing stores (formal sector businesses) in central Ho Chi Minh City (HCMC). The stores were located in the following districts/streets: Nguyen Trai, Le Van Sy, Ngo Nhon Tinh, Nguyen Van Dau, Le Quang Dinh, Ly Thuong Kiet, Hoang Van Thu, and Nguyen Dinh. The sample group of small firms employed 4-15 workers. Sixty (60) percent of owners had been in business for more than 10 years; 80 percent had started the business themselves, while the remaining 20 percent succeeded the business from their parents;

77 percent were female; 73 percent were over 30 years of age; and, 80 percent had high school education only.

Data were collected in August-September 2009, using a qualitative approach by way of semi-structured interviews. The interview schedule included questions on business characteristics, owner demographics, employees, perceptions about the impact of the global economic recession, and views regarding other local factors that affect the efficiency of business operations. The interviews were conducted in the Vietnamese language; responses were recorded in writing, and then translated into English by research assistants. On average, interviews lasted about 20 minutes.

Results

All respondents to the present study recognised the impact of the global economic recession on company sales. Respondents reported that January-August 2009 sales had declined by 20-50 percent (average 32 percent) over the same period for 2008. These figures are consistent with other studies in other Asian countries subject to the global economic recession (see, for example, Egan & Tosanguan 2009 for the case of small firms in Thailand). In an attempt to cope with the decline in sales, the respondents to the present study used sales discounts (30-50 percent) to increase cash flow, and reduced costs by reducing the amount of inventory. No respondent mentioned employee layoffs as a response to the recessionary effects.

All respondents to the study owned the shop from which they operated their businesses. 83 percent of the respondents to the study reported that the start-up of their businesses was financed with personal capital. The other 17 percent utilised 'personal networks' to obtain the required capital. This finding is indicative of the general problem of the limited access to finance for small business owners as observed by other authors (for example, Asian Development Bank 2009b; Farrell and Downing 1997; Rand 2007; Thomsen 2007).

The respondents reported that the most serious business constraints, beyond the immediacy of the global economic recession, were (in rank order of significance):

1. Strong competition
2. Government taxes
3. Poor infrastructure

The most serious concern for the clothing retailers of HCMC was the high level of competition. For example, numerous clothing retailers are located next to each other on Nguyen Trai and Le Van Sy streets offering various choices to customers. The second most significant concern was tax burden. Respondents said they were subject to four different taxes; income tax, license tax, rental income tax, and pavement charge. For instance, one typical shop owner paid out US$390 per month for the four taxes, including US$150 income tax, US$15 license tax, US$180 rental income tax, and US$45 pavement charge. Rental income tax was reported to vary by type of business, with retail clothing suffering a higher tax burden than other merchandise retail. The third most significant challenge for small firms in HCMC was poor infrastructure. The most vocal respondents on this issue owned shops in Le Van Sy Street where roadworks in front of their shops had been in progress for over two months. The roadworks had caused traffic jams, and discouraged customers. In addition, the roadworks had exacerbated poor drainage, and hence, caused flooding whenever there was heavy rain.

In order to address the issue of competition, 77 percent of the respondents focused on customer service; for example, salespersons often offered special prices for loyal customers, and contacted them when there were new arrivals. The remainder of the respondents (23 percent) reported that they competed on price alone. Many also sought suppliers who could provide them with attractive clothing styles.

In addition to the most serious constraints on their businesses and the effects of the economic recession, the business owners were also asked about some of the management practices that they employed. The respondents generally reported that they perceived their primary function as managing day-to-day operations in a very hands-on manner. The implication of their view of management was that they felt it necessary to be present at their shop for as many of the opening hours as possible. For those opening hours when the owners could not be physically present, they tended to delegate to family members or relatives on whom they believed they could rely. On the issue of recruitment, respondents generally suggested that high school education was not a prerequisite for employment. The more important issues being neat appearance, and experience in sales. None of the small firms used any form of performance appraisal for their employees. Owners instead observed salespersons during work time, and provided comments immediately when someone did "something wrong"; that is, a reliance on negative reinforcement to condition behaviour (Skinner 1969). None of the respondents provided formal training for employees, but they did informally induct new employees on the basics of shop rules, prices, and origin of merchandise.

On the issue of compensation practices, full-time salespersons earned on average US$60 per month (2 million Vietnamese Dong), and received an additional US$15 bonus on the Tet holiday (3-day lunar new year festival; January-February). Part-time salespersons earned on average US$35 per month, and received no bonus on the Tet holiday. The wages of full-time retail sales staff, while more than the average income of US$30 per month for urban dwellers in Vietnam (Vietnam Household Living Standards Survey: Income 2006), were considerably less than alternative employment choices, such as clothing factory workers who could earn US$100 per month (Vietnam garment makers face rising bankruptcies 2006).

Discussion and Conclusions

The study sought to explore the short-term impact of the 2008 global economic recession, as well as the longer-term business constraints that impact on the efficiency and potential for growth for small firms in Vietnam. To this end, the study focused on the retail clothing industry in Ho Chi Minh City (HCMC) as a basic barometer of the health of the Vietnamese economy.

The results of the study highlight a number of common characteristics of Vietnamese small firms. These characteristics include family-ownership, distrust of outsiders, strong competition, and lack of managerial skills. There appears to be a vicious circle involving owners employing uneducated workers on low wages, and low productivity of both employees, and owners whose time is consumed with close supervision amidst a distrustful working environment.

The results support the views of other authors that human resource management in small Vietnamese firms is ineffective, in terms of selection, motivation, performance appraisal, training, and compensation practices (see, for example, Hiemstra et al. 2006; King-Kauanui et al. 2006; Mansurel and Smit 2000; Nguyen 2007; Nguyen et al. 2004). Limited access to finance was raised indirectly by the fact that all respondents had financed the start-up of their businesses with either personal funds, or funds from their 'personal network' of relatives or contacts. Operating costs were problematic in the form of government taxes. Rental costs were not an issue because all respondents owned the commercial premises from which they operated their businesses. Indeed, the ownership of premises provided a great deal of resilience in the economic recession, saving them from the fate of bankruptcy that had befallen many other Vietnamese businesses in 2008 (Phuoc 2009).

Moreover, small firms naturally have the advantage of flexibility in the control of inventory, as well as intimate contact with customers, each again providing some resilience in challenging economic times.

The results of the study indicate that the infrastructure of HCMC is not particularly conducive to the business environment. Traffic jams, deteriorated roads, and frequent flooding are unfavourable experiences to the Vietnamese in general, and to family-based small firms in particular.

The business constraints identified by the present study are, of course, not unique to Vietnam. Indeed, issues such as lack of access to finance, complex and corrupt government administration, poor infrastructure, and lowly educated human resources are synonymous with less developed countries (see, for example, Chowdhury 2007; Egan 2009; Kellow 2007; Robson and Obeng 2007; UNCTAD 2006; UNCTAD 2007). Despite substantial government intervention on behalf of small business since 2000, the results of the study indicate that much more institutional reform and expenditure on human resources and infrastructure is required if Vietnam is to continue on the path of economic development.

References

Asian Development Bank. 2009a. *Enterprises in Asia: Fostering Dynamism in SMEs*. Retrieved August 30, 2009 from http://www.adb.org

—. 2009b. *Socialist Republic of Viet Nam: Subprogram II of the Small and Medium Enterprise Development Program Cluster*. Retrieved August 30, 2009 from http://www.adb.org

Bleaney, M. & Nishiyama, A. 2002. Explaining growth: A contest between models. *Journal of Economic Growth*. 7:43-56

Burns, P. 2007. *Entrepreneurship and Small Business*. 2nd ed. New York: Palgrave Macmillan

Central bank, economists discuss interest rate subsidies. 2009. Retrieved October 13, 2009 from http://english.vietnamnet.vn

Chowdhury, S.M. 2007. Overcoming entrepreneurship development constraints: The case of Bangladesh. *Journal of Enterprises Communities*. 1(3):240-251

Costs of doing business in Vietnam ranks no.1 in the region 2008. Retrieved September 10, 2009 from http://www.namdinhvu.com [in Vietnamese]

Daniels, L. & Mead, D.C. 1998. The contribution of small enterprises to household and national income in Kenya. *Economic Development and Cultural Change*. 47(1):45-71

Decree about developing SMEs 2009. Retrieved August 20, 2009 from http://hoichothuongmai.com [in Vietnamese]

Denney, S. 2008. *Labor & Education: Vietnam's Human Resources Quality Ranks 11th in Asia.* World Bank. Vietnam News Briefs

Discount garments fail to find buyers 2008. *Vietnamnet*, November 17. Retrieved August 30, 2009 from http://english.vietnamnet.vn

Domestic fashion: Weaknesses in distribution and designing stage 2008. Retrieved September 20, 2009 from http://www.thesaigontimes.vn [in Vietnamese]

Egan, V. 2009. Environmental Constraints on Small Enterprises in Tanzania: A Case Study of the Retail Electrical, Retail Clothing, and Travel Industries in Dar es Salaam. *Proceedings of the 2009 International Academy of African American Business (IAABD)*, Kampala, Uganda 19-23 May

Egan, V. & Tosanguan, P. 2009. Coping Strategies of Entrepreneurs in Economic Recession: A Comparative Analysis of Thais and European Expatriates in Pattaya, Thailand. *Journal of Asia Entrepreneurship and Sustainability*. December. 17-36

Farrell, B.R. & Downing, J.R. 1997. Doing business in Vietnam. *CPA Journal*. 66(4)

Gould, B. 2008. Who voted for the markets? *The Guardian*. November 26. Retrieved November 12, 2009 from http://www.guardian.co.uk

Harvie, C. & Lee, B-C. 2002. East Asian SMEs: Contemporary issues and developments-An overview. In C.Harvie & B.-C.Lee (Eds.). *The Role of SMEs in National Economies in East Asia*. Cheltenham: Edward Elgar. 1-20

Hiemstra, A.M.F., van der Kooy, K.G. & Frese, M. 2006. Entrepreneurship in the street food sector of Vietnam – Assessment of Psychological success and failure factors. *Journal of Small Business Management*. 44(3):474-481

High operating expenses limit capablilities attracting investment 2005. Retrieved September 10, 2009 from http://tintuc.xalo.vn [in Vietnamese]

Hong, V. 2009. Banks maintain loans for small enterprises. *The Saigon Times*, January 1. Retrieved August 30, 2009 from http://english.thesaigontimes.vn

IMF 2009. *World Economic Outlook: Sustaining the Recovery*. International Monetary Fund. Retrieved November 222, 2009 from http://imf.org

Karkoviata, L. 2001. Getting down to business. *Asian Business*. 37(8):46-48

Kellow, N. 2007. *Investment Climate and Competitiveness: Improving Access to Finance.* World Bank. Washington. Retrieved April 16, 2009 from http://www.worldbank.org

King-Kauanui, S., Su, N.D. & Ashley-Cotleur, C. 2006. Impact of Human Resource Management: SME performance in Vietnam. *Journal of Development Entrepreneurship.* 11(1):79-97

Klapper, L. & Delgado, J.M.Q. 2007. *Entrepreneurship.* Viewpoint Series. Note 316. World Bank. Financial and Private Sector Development Vice Presidency. Washington. Retrieved April 16, 2009 from http://www.worldbank.org

Kokko, A. & Sjoholm, F. 2006. The internationalization of Vietnamese small and medium-size enterprises. *Asian Economic Papers.* 4(1):152-177

Krugman, P. 2008. The Madoff economy. *The New York Times.* December 19. Retrieved November 19, 2009 from http://www.nytimes.com

Loftus, M. 2008. Economist discusses causes of global economic downturn. *America.gov.* November 14. Retrieved October 20, 2009 from http://www.america.gov

Lombra, R. 2009. The U.S. Financial Crisis: Global Repercussions. *Junior Achievement.* Retrieved September 20, 2009 from http://www.ja.org

Mansurel, E. & Smit, H.P. 2000. Planning behavior of small firms in central Vietnam. *Journal of Small Business Management.* 38(2):95-102

Many SMEs will go into bankruptcy 2009. Retrieved August 30, 2009 from http://www.chicuctdcbinhthuan.gov.vn [in Vietnamese]

Meyer, K. E., Tran, Y.T.T. & Nguyen, H.V. 2006. Doing Business in Vietnam. *Thunderbird International Business Review.* 48(2):263-290

Ngo, C. 2006. Despite many reforms, doing business is still not easy in Vietnam. *Business Issues Bulletin.* 11(4):1-4. Retrieved August 30, 2009 from http://www.ifc.org

Nguyen, T.P. 2008. *Administrative procedures' reforms in providing business license today.* Retrieved September 20, 2009 from http://thongtinphapluatdansu.wordpress.com [in Vietnamese]

Nguyen, V.B. 2009. Moving towards a Post-Crisis World. *Paper presented at the 5th Asia-Europe Journalists' Seminar.* Asia-Europe Foundation. 23-24 May. Hanoi, Vietnam

Nguyen, V.T. & Bryant, S.E. 2004. A Study of the Formality of Human Resource Management Practices in Small and Medium-Size Enterprises in Vietnam. *International Small Business Journal.* 22(6):595-618

Nguyen, Y.U. 2007. *The Determinants of Retail Performance in Vietnam.* Unpublished Dissertation of the Degree of Master of Business

Administration. University of the Thai Chamber of Commerce (UTCC), Bangkok, Thailand.

OECD 2009. *OECD Economic Outlook.* No.86. November. Retrieved November 21, 2009 from http://www.oecd.org

Phan, M.N. 2008a. Sources of Vietnam's economic growth. *Progress in Development Studies.* 8(3):209-29

—. 2008b. The roles of capital and technological progress in Vietnam's economic growth. *Journal of Economic Studies.* 35(2):200-215

Phuoc, H. 2009. 7,000 SMEs bankrupt amid global crisis. *Vietnamnet,* March 19. Retrieved September 30, 2009 from http://english.vietnamnet.vn

Pincus, J. 2009. Vietnam Sustaining Growth in Difficult Times. *ASEAN Economic Bulletin.* 26(1):11-24

Ramachandran, V. & Shah, M.K. 1999. Minority entrepreneurs and firm performance in Sub-Saharan Africa. *Journal of Development Studies.* 36(2):71-87

Rand, J. 2007. Credit Constraints and Determinants of the Cost of Capital in Vietnamese Manufacturing. *Small Business Economics.* 29(1):1-13

Robson, A.J.P. & Obeng, A.B. 2007. The barriers to growth in Ghana. *Small Business Economics.* 30(4):385-403

Shah, A. 2009. *Global Financial Crisis.* Global Issues. Retrieved November 24, 2009 from http://www.globalissues.org

Skinner, B.F. 1969. *Contingencies of Reinforcement.* New York: Appleton-Century-Crofts

Small and medium enterprises' week to launch in Hanoi. 2008. *VietNamNet,* October 15. Retrieved August 30, 2009 from http://english.vietnamnet.vn

SMEs vital for economy, but short of cash. 2009. *Vietnam Economic Portal.* Retrieved August 30, 2009 from http://www.vnep.org.vn

Solving problems facing Vietnamese SMEs 2008. Retrieved September 30, 2009 from http://www.agro.gov.vn [in Vietnamese]

Spencer, J.W. & Gomez, C. 2004. The relationship among national institutional structures, economic factors, and domestic entrepreneurial activity: A multicountry study. *Journal of Business Research.* 57:1098-1107

Thomsen, L. 2007. Accessing global value chains: The role of business-state relations in the private clothing industry in Vietnam. *Journal of Economic Geography.* 7:753–776

Tran. T.C., Le, S.X. & Nguyen, A.K. 2008. Vietnam's small- and medium-sized enterprises development: Characteristics, constraints and policy recommendations. Retrieved August 30, 2009 from http://www.eria.org

Transportation Infrastructure Development in Vietnam 2009. Vietnam National Committee On Large Dams and Water Resources Development. Retrieved August 30, 2009 from http://www.vncold.vn

UNCTAD 2006. *The Least Developed Countries Report, 2006.* United Nations Conference on Trade and Development. Geneva. Retrieved April 20, 2009 from www.unctad.org

—. 2007. *The Least Developed Countries Report, 2007.* United Nations Conference on Trade and Development. Geneva. Retrieved April 20, 2009 from www.unctad.org

UPS Snapshot for Small Businesses: Doing business in Vietnam 2008. Retrieved August 25, 2009 from http://compass.ups.com

van Praag, C.M. & Versloot, P.H. 2007. What is the value of entrepreneurship? A review of recent research. *Small Business Economics.* 29(4):351-382

VBF 2007, *Report on Business Environment Sentiment Survey,* Vietnam Business Forum

Vietnam: An On-The-Ground Perspective. 2009. *Emerging Markets Monitor.* 15(1):1-3

Vietnam coping with global recession "reasonably well" - ADB economist 2009. *BBC Monitoring Asia Pacific,* July 12

Vietnam economy: Education is a major concern 2009. *EIU ViewsWire.* 11 June

Vietnam garment makers face rising bankruptcies 2006. *The Financial Express.* August 31. Retrieved November 21, 2009 from http://www.financialexpress.com

Vietnam Household Living Standards Survey: Income 2006. *General Statistics Office of Vietnam (GSOV).* Retrieved November 20, 2009 from http://www.gso.gov.vn

Vietnam loses clothing-market share 2008. *Vietnamnet,* September 22. Retrieved September 20, 2009 from http://english.vietnamnet.vn

Vietnam retail analysis (2008-2012) 2008. Retrieved August 20, 2009 from http://www.vinase.com

Vietnamese retailers brace themselves for the inevitable 2008. Retrieved October 21, 2009 from http://tintuc.xalo.vn

Wickham, J. 2009. Jobs and investment industry snapshot – Retail therapy. *Victorian Employers' Chamber of Commerce (VECCI).* June 25, 2009. Retrieved November 17, 2009 from http://www.vecci.org.au

World Bank 1993. *The East Asian Miracle: Economic Growth and Public Policy.* New York: Oxford University

CHAPTER EIGHT

A COMPARISON OF BRAND EQUITY ELEMENTS FOR CONVENTIONAL AND SHARIA BANKS IN INDONESIA

MA'MUN SARMA AND MARTHIN G. NANERE

Abstract

The purpose of this paper is to analyse and compare brand equity between sharia and conventional banks. More specifically, the objectives of this paper are to analyze brand awareness, brand association, perceived quality and brand loyalty between sharia and conventional banks. Looking at brand equity the findings suggest that in terms of brand awareness, the sharia bank has been better known compared to the counterpart. Sharia and conventional banks have fulfilled the same brand association criteria. However, in perceived quality element, conventional banks have been rated from sufficient to very good, whereas sharia banks from sufficient to good only. Regarding brand loyalty, it appears that the percentage of committed buyers of sharia banks is higher than that for the counterpart. Based on this outcome, the article concludes by proposing recommendations on marketing strategy for sharia banks in Indonesia.

Introduction

Indonesia is one of the ASEAN members ranked fourth in the world by population size, and is also the largest Muslim country. Indonesia is also blessed with a richness of natural resources, such as forest and ocean, and also mineral resources such as copper, coal and petroleum. However, Indonesia is facing a poverty problem. In addition, the Human Development Index (HDI) of Indonesia is left far behind that of Singapore and Malaysia, and indeed, also now Vietnam's HDI is superior to Indonesia. Why has this happened?

Indonesia's economy is dominated by the micro, small and medium enterprises (MSMEs). In 2007, the number of MSMEs and big enterprise is 48.97 million, whereas the number of big and medium enterprises is only 7,000 and 106,000, respectively (Departemen Perdagangan RI 2009). The number of micro and small enterprises is 4.2 million and 44.6 million, respectively, thus the percentage of micro and small enterprises is 99.77 percent. Furthermore, the contribution of micro and small enterprises to GDP is 53.6 percent, and the number of worker employed by these enterprises is 91.8 million. In summary, the micro and small enterprise sector is almost 100 percent by number, and also absorbs a huge number or worker, but the contribution from these enterprises to the economy is only 54 percent.

Sharia economics has been viewed as a solution to overcome the poverty problem, unemployment, and lack of education. Based on the fact that the Indonesian economy is dominated by MSMEs, the role of sharia economics is highly respected for Indonesian economy development. One of the roles of a Sharia economy is to improve the profile of Sharia bank to assist the financial problems faced by MSMEs. Sharia banking in Indonesia has grown significantly since its implementation in 1992. In 1998, sharia banking was legitimized with the formal launching of the dual banking system (that is, sharia and conventional banking).

Table 1 shows the growth in total assets of sharia and conventional banks during the period 2005 to 2010. The total assets of sharia banks (Islamic Commercial Bank and Islamic Business Unit Condensed Balance Sheet) are valued at 21-98 trillion rupiah (US$2.3-10.9bn), while conventional banks are valued at 1,298-2,601 trillion rupiah (US$144.2-289). Based on total assets, sharia banks are relatively small compared to conventional banks. Table 1 shows that the percentage of the total assets of sharia banks to conventional banks is 1.61-3.77 percent, or an average of 2.41 percent. In 2011, the number of sharia bank offices was 1,763, up from 550 in 2005. Based on this phenomenon, the total assets of the sharia banks should increase higher than that performed today. This is due to the percentage of Muslim's in the Indonesian population, being about 85 percent or 190 million. The assets of sharia banks has grown annually 28.57-48.49 percent, or by an average of 36.24 percent. Meanwhile, conventional banks have only grown 0.18 percent average. During the Global Financial Crisis commencing in 2008, sharia banks demonstrated less sensitivity compared to conventional banks.

The purpose of this paper is to generally analyse brand equity between sharia and conventional banks. More specifically, the objectives of this paper are to analyze brand awareness, brand association, perceived quality, and brand loyalty between sharia and conventional banks. The paper will also propose several recommendations in the hope of increasing the contribution of the sharia banks in the development of the Indonesian economy.

This article is structured into 5 sections. The next section will discuss the theoretical background and conceptual framework, followed by methodology and discussion sections. The final section outlines the conclusions and recommendations.

Table 1: The Total Assets of Sharia Banks and Conventional Banks in Indonesia (2005-2010)

Banking Assets	2005	2006	2007	2008	2009	2010	Ave
Shariah Bank (Trillion Rp)[1]	21	27	37	50	66	98	
Growth (%)		28.6	37.0	35.1	32.0	48.5	36.2
Conventional Bank (Trillion Rp)[2]	1,298	1,489	2,013	2,016	2,210	2,601	
Growth (%)		14.7	35.2	0.2	9.6	17.7	17.4
Percentage of the total asset of the sharia bank to the conventional bank (%)	1.6	1.81	1.8	2.5	3.0	3.8	2.4

Notes:
[1]Bank of Indonesia 2011a: Islamic Banking Statistic, January 2011 (Table 6: Islamic Commercial Bank and Islamic Business Unit Condensed Balance Sheet).
[2]Bank of Indonesia 2011b: Indonesian Banking Statistic, Vol. 9, No. 2, January 2011 (Table 1: Bank industries operation; Total asset consists of commercial banks and rural banks).

Theoretical Background and Conceptual Framework

The Indonesian dual banking system (i.e., sharia and conventional banking) was launched formally in 1998. There is one major difference between sharia and conventional banks (Santoso & Triandaru 2006):
1. Sharia bank is a bank in which the activities of collecting and allocating funds are based on Islamic principles, such as trading and profit sharing. Rent or usury is prohibited in Islam.

2. Conventional bank is a bank in which the activities of collecting and allocating funds are in the form of rent, or in a certain percentage from the fund for a certain time period.

Kotler (2000, p.404) suggests that a brand is not only a symbol, design or a sign that does not have a meaning, but a brand is also an identity of a product, whereas customers are able to differentiate the products or services that the customers are willing to buy. Therefore, a brand is an important asset to a business, and is characterized in terms of intangible and tangible benefits.

Aaker (1991) defines brand equity as a set of brand assets and liabilities linked to a brand; its name and symbol that add to or subtract from the value provided by a product or service to a firm/or to that firm's customers. Assets and liabilities of the brand equity will be different from context to context. However, the brand equity element can be grouped into five elements, including brand awareness, perceived quality, brand associations, brand loyalty, and other proprietary brand assets.

Furthermore, Aaker (1996) proposes 'brand equity ten' to measure the most effective and tracking brand equity over products and markets. The brand equity ten consists of ten sets of measures grouped into five categories; the first four categories represent customer perceptions of the brand along the four dimensions of brand equity, loyalty measures (price premium and satisfaction/loyalty), perceived quality/leadership measures (perceived quality and leadership), associations/differentiation measures (perceived value, brand personality and organizational associations) and awareness measures (brand awareness). The fifth category includes two sets of market behavior (market share and price measured representing information obtained from market information rather than directly from customers).

Moisescu and Allen (2010) suggest that the concept of brand loyalty and equity has been discussed from a variety of perspective. The concept was originally proposed by Aaker (1991), and further developed by Travis (2000) and Keller (2008). This study will employ brand equity elements as proposed by Aaker (1991) from the perspective of consumers; namely brand awareness, perceived quality, brand associations, and brand loyalty. The conceptual framework of the study is presented in Figure 1.

Methodology

Location and Time
The location of the study was in the city of Bogor, West Java Province (for a sharia bank) and Makassar, South Sulawesi (for a conventional

bank). The city of Bogor was chosen as representative of Java island, while Makassar was representative of outside of Java. The location and the name of the sharia and conventional banks were selected purposively. The data were collected during the period of April-May 2009 in the city of Bogor, and July-August 2009 in Makassar.

Sampling Procedure

The sampling procedure was based on accidental sampling, which is non-probability sampling. The number of sample was calculated by Slovin formula with 10 percent error. The total number of respondents was 200.

Figure 1: Conceptual Framework of the Study

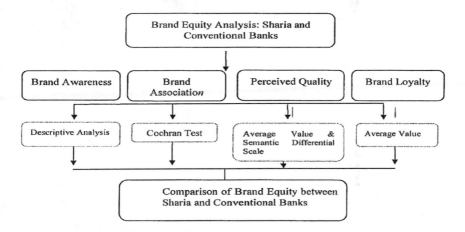

Definition of Operational Variables

The operational variables used in this article are defined as follows:

1. Brand Awareness is the ability of consumers to recognise and remember that a brand belongs to a certain category. The measurement of brand awareness can be categorised into four levels, namely brand unaware, brand recall, brand recognition, and top of mind. Descriptive analysis was employed for this variable.

2. Brand association relates to everything that could be related directly or indirectly toward a brand based on consumers' memory that can be performed by the impression of the brand in relation to consumers habitual, life style, product attributes, geography, price, competitors and celebrities. The brand association is measured by brand strength, brand favorability, and brand uniqueness. Cochran

test was employed to this variable to examine the significance of the relationship of its association in a brand, and the association that is related will perform a brand image of the brand.

3. Perceived quality is Consumers' perception towards overall quality or excellence of a product or services. The measurement of perceived quality was based on product and service dimensions. The average score and semantic differential scale were employed for this variable.

4. Brand loyalty is the level of consumers' commitment to a brand, shown by higher frequency of the brand compared to other brands for the same product. Brand loyalty is measured by switcher buyer, habitual buyer, satisfied buyer, liking the brand and committed buyer. Descriptive analysis was employed to this variable.

Validity and Reliability

The appropriate data were examined for their validity and reliability. Validity was examined by Product Moment Pearson, and reliability was examined by Spearman Brown and Cronbach Alpha. The reliability test for brand association shows the data are reliable based on Spearman Brown; r calculation is greater than r table based on 95 percent confidence level for both sharia and conventional banks. The validity test for perceived quality shows the data are valid; r calculation is greater than r table based on 95 percent confidence level for both sharia and conventional banks. In addition, the reliability test for perceived quality shows the data are reliable based on Cronbach Alpha; sharia bank 0.913, and conventional bank 0.910.

Results and Discussion

The majority of respondents were 21-30 years of age, followed by 31-40 years, above 40 years and below 21 years. The education of the respondents is majority Bachelor, followed by Senior High School only, and Junior High School graduates. The monthly expenditure is dominated by 1-3 million rupiah (US$110-330). The majority of respondents received information about sharia and conventional banks from colleagues and family members, followed by printed material and newspapers, brochures/leaflet, advertisements, and the Internet.

Brand Awareness

The brand awareness elements in this study are brand unawareness, brand recall, brand recognition, and top of mind. All respondents of both sharia and conventional banks were aware of the banks selected in this study. In addition, all respondents of both sharia and conventional banks also recognised the banks that were selected for this study without assistance.

In relation to the brand recall, the sharia bank was mentioned as the first bank by 64 percent of respondents, but the conventional bank was mentioned as the fourth bank by 24 percent of respondents. However, based on top of mind criterion, sharia bank was only declared by 52 percent of respondents, while the conventional bank was declared by 60 percent.

Brand Association

Respondents were asked everything that could be related directly or indirectly toward a brand based on consumers' memory that can be performed by the impression of the brand in relation to consumers habitual, life style, product attributes, geography, price, competitors and celebrities. There are 10 statements asked to respondents of both for sharia and conventional banks. There were four statements that were not the same for the sharia and conventional banks due to the nature of difference between those banks. Up to 10 statements, based on Cochrane test, the sharia bank rated highly on only 5 statements: (1) pure sharia bank; (2) guaranteed halal; (3) Islamic atmosphere; (4) employees are sincere and friendly; and, (5) the system is more fair. However, the conventional bank rated highly on 7 statements: (1) high technology bank; (2) professional;, (3) growth of the bank is relatively good; (4) branch offices are everywhere; (5) ATM network is scattered widely; (6) employees are sincere and friendly; and, (7) variety of products.

Perceived Quality

Likert scale and Semantic differential scale were employed to analyse perceived quality of the sharia and conventional banks by the respondents. A 5-point Likert scale was used, ranging from strongly agree (5) to strongly disagree (1). The Semantic differential scale used bipolar statements according to the following:

- Bad   Very good
- Slow   Very fast
- Weak   Very strong
- Passive Active

There are 17 attributes of perceived quality, but there are three attributes that are not the same for the sharia and conventional banks due to the different nature of those banks. For sharia banks, the average score of the attribute of perceived quality was between 3.29 (easiness and fast transaction) and 4.17 (guaranteed halal). However, for the conventional bank the score was between 2.99 (the amount of the first deposit) and 4.39 (ATM network). This means that the perceived quality of sharia bank ranges between sufficient to good, but for the conventional bank it is between sufficient to very good.

Brand Loyalty

Brand loyalty was measured by switcher buyer, habitual buyer, satisfied buyer, liking the brand and committed buyer. The five components of the brand loyalty were expected to be an upside down pyramid, this means the switcher buyer is the least percentage, followed by habitual buyer, satisfied buyer, liking the brand, and committed buyer whereas the committed buyer is the biggest percentage. The results indicate that the pattern of brand royalty of sharia bank does not tend to be an upside down pyramid, unlike the conventional bank. Interestingly, brand loyalty for the sharia bank is relatively low compared to that of the conventional bank. The number of loyal customers of sharia bank is only 14 percent compared to the conventional bank of 44 percent.

Proposed Marketing Strategy for Sharia Bank

Brand loyalty is viewed as one of the most important elements of the brand equity (Moisescu & Allen 2010). A bank's marketing strategy should be more focused on brand loyalty, especially for the sharia bank. As mentioned before, Indonesia is the largest Muslim country in the world, but the role of the sharia bank (in terms of total assets) is only about 3 percent even though the sharia bank has been established since 1998.

Abduh (2011), in his research on service quality in sharia banks, asked the respondents about five service dimensions of Islamic banking (reliability, tangibles, rates and charges, bank-customer relationship, and sharia), and how those dimensions impact their propensity to withdraw their deposit if the service quality of the bank is bad. The results indicated that people would withdraw their deposits if the service quality is bad toward sharia (60.1 percent), followed by tangibles (54.7 percent), rents and charges (27.5 percent), reliability (26.8 percent), and customer-bank relationship (11.3 percent). The main reason respondents would withdraw their deposits is that if the service quality in relation to sharia is bad. If the sharia bank does not fulfill the sharia law, this will bring the customers to withdraw their deposits. For the sharia bank's customers, this is a very logical reason. The customers deposit their money to sharia bank because the sharia bank is guaranteed halal.

Based on brand loyalty finding from this research, and Abduh's (2011) finding as mentioned above, marketing strategy for sharia banks may be proposed. To obtain high loyalty from the customers, it is required a relatively long period of time. In fact, the sharia bank has been established for almost 20 years. Parallel with the period of establishment and also the increase of the sharia bank offices, this will improve the brand loyalty. In addition, the sharia aspect as part of the sharia bank services should be maintained and improved. The sharia aspect should be treated as an entry point to increase brand loyalty.

In the establishment of a marketing strategy, generally referred to will be marketing mix, comprises the 4-Ps (Product, Price, Promotion and Place); although this marketing strategy is more common for products, than services. Lovelock and Wirtz (2007) propose 8-Ps which consists of Product elements, Place and time, Price and other user outlays, Promotion and education, Process, Physical environment, People, and Productivity and quality. The products of sharia banks are services, thus to obtain success in marketing, sharia banks are recommended to adopt the 8-P approach. In addition, since sharia banks should pertain to sharia law, sharia principles should also be integrated into the marketing strategy. The sharia bank should advise their customers that all activities of the bank conform to sharia laws and principles.

The prospects for sharia banks are promising, based on growth of assets, and the number of existing offices. However, the role of the bank in the economy is still relatively weak when compared to the number of Muslims in Indonesia. Given the huge number of MSMEs in Indonesia, the role of the sharia bank could be expected to be highly significant.

Conclusions and Recommendations

This study has discussed five components of brand equity of the sharia and conventional banks. Brand equity of sharia and conventional banks demonstrate differences. In terms of brand awareness, the sharia bank has is better known in Indonesia compared to conventional banks. Sharia and conventional banks have fulfilled the same brand association criteria. However, in perceived quality element, sharia banks have been rated from sufficient to good only, whereas conventional banks have been rated from sufficient to very good. Regarding brand loyalty, it appears that the percentage of committed buyers of sharia banks is lower than that for the conventional banks. This study recommends that sharia banks implement the 8-P approach to marketing strategy, but tempered by sharia principles.

References

Aaker, D.A. 1991. *Managing Brand Equity: Capitalizing on the Value of a Brand Name*. New York: Free Press

—. 1996. Measuring brand equity across products and markets. *California Management Review.* 38(3):102-120

Abduh, M. 2011. Islamic banking service quality and withdrawal risk: The Indonesian experience. *International Journal of Excellence in Islamic Banking and Finance.* 1(2)

Bank of Indonesia 2011a. *Islamic Banking Statistic.* January

—. 2011b. *Indonesian Banking Statistic.* 9(2). January

Departemen Perdagangan RI 2009. Promosi Ekspor: PKL dan Produl Lokal Sumbar. *Media Perdagangan* Edisi. 03/2009:36-38 [in Indonesian]

Kotler, P. 2000. *Marketing Management: The Millennium Edition.* New Jersey: Prentice-Hall

Lovelock, C. & Wirtz, J. 2007. *Services Marketing: People, Technology, Strategy.* 6th Ed. New Jersey: Prentice-Hall

Moisescu, O.I. & Allen, B. 2010. The relationship between the dimensions of brand loyalty: An empirical investigation among Romanian urban consumers. *Management & Marketing Challenges for Knowledge Society.* 5(4):83-98

Santoso, B.T & Triandaru, T. 2006. *Bank dan Lembaga Keuangan Lain.* Jakarta: Salemba Empat [in Indonesian]

CHAPTER NINE

A CASE STUDY OF UBON RATCHATHANI RICE FARMERS: THE THAI GOVERNMENT'S RESPONSIBILITY IN SUPPORTING THE EXPORT OF RICE

RACHAYA INDANON

Abstract

Thailand is the biggest rice exporter in the world market. However, Thai farmers (i.e., the rice producers) receive less financial benefits from the continuously increasing price of the rice products. Most of the farmers do not export by themselves. According to the research survey, more than 90 percent of the farmers in Ubon Ratchathani (province in Thailand) do not have the knowledge and ability to export. This case study highlights what the Thai government should do to support Thai farmers so that they might receive more benefits from exporting their rice. The results show that the Thai government can act as a key organization to fairly allocate benefits among stakeholders, such as farmers, middlemen, and exporting companies along with the rice private organizations. The Thai government also should integrate the different government sectors to smoothly enhance the farmers' productivity and quality.

Introduction

North-Eastern Thailand is an important area for the production of rice, a significant agricultural product for the country in terms of consumption and export. It is also a major source of high quality rice such as Jasmine rice for export (Wijnhoud, Konboon & Lefroy 2003). In 2006, Ubon Ratchathani, a province in this area, produced 11.88 tons of good quality Jasmine rice from 24,764 rai of land. Leading areas of Jasmine rice production in Ubon Ratchathani were Kudkhawpun, Muangsamsib,

Dechudom, Buntharic, Sumrong, Piboonmungsahan, Trakanpudpon, Srimungmai, Nayia, and Luasuacoke (Theerapongthanakorn 2006).

Jasmine rice (Thai *Hom Mali*) is a soft, fragrant, delicious rice popular domestically and internationally, and according to the Ministry of Agriculture, represents 40.22 percent of Thailand's exported rice in 2006. Its export is worth more than 20,000 million baht per year (Krungthepthurakit 2007). Major export markets are the EU, US, Canada, Africa, China, Hong Kong, Malaysia, Taiwan, Brunei, and Singapore. Jasmine rice for export accounted for 40 percent per year of total production, and the rest was for domestic consumption. Jasmine rice from Ubon Ratchathani constituted the highest proportion of rice for export.

Foreign demand for Thai Jasmine rice increased from 60,282 million baht in 2008 to 68,578 baht in 2009, a rise of 13.76 percent in one year.

Table 1: Thailand's export of Jasmine rice (Million Baht)

2004	2005	2006	2007	2008	2009
35,572	34,904	40,341	47,988	60,282	68,578

Source: Office of Agricultural Economics (OAE), Ministry of Agriculture and Cooperatives, Thailand

Although the export market continues to grow, Thai farmers receive few benefits. Most do not export by themselves and even in Ubon Ratchathani, an area with an integrated network of agricultural workers and rice mill associations, exports are via middlemen or export companies. Only one agricultural institution in Ubon Ratchathani, the Progressive Farmers Association in Trakanpudpon district, handles its own export affairs.

This case study investigated ways in which the Thai government can assist Thai farmers to receive more benefits from exporting rice. The study had four specific objectives. The primary objective was to compare farmer groups involved in direct export with those involved in indirect export. The second objective was to examine factors related to Ubon Ratchathani farmer groups' capability in exporting Jasmine rice. Examples of these factors were production costs and efficiency, financial funds in marketing operation, export knowledge, and export capability. The third objective was to investigate problems of and obstacles to Ubon Ratchathani farmer groups in exporting Jasmine rice. The final objective was to study government support for Thai farmers to receive more benefits from exporting the rice.

The following section provides an overview of Ubon Ratchthani farmers' institutions, Thailand rice production, the rice market, competition in the world rice market, and rice exporters' government policy, theories, and conceptual framework. Section 3 demonstrates methodology. Section 4 shows the results of the case study. Finally, section 5 presents discussion and conclusion.

Overview

Farmers' Institutions

Farmers' institutions in Ubon Ratchathani are classified into agricultural groups and cooperative agricultural groups. Some of the agricultural groups coordinate and cooperate with entrepreneurs, while others have their own rice mills.

Table 2: Farmers' Institutions

Classification	No.	Responsible Unit
Agricultural groups	100	Office of Agriculture
Cooperative agricultural groups	47	Office of Cooperatives

Source: Office of Agriculture, Ubon Ratchathani; Office of Cooperatives, Ubon Ratchathani, 2010

Rice Production

North-Eastern Thailand is responsible for the production of 82 percent of Thailand's Jasmine rice. The most important provinces are Ubon Ratchathani, Amnat Chareon, Roi-Et, Yasothorn, and Srisaket (Economic Agricultural Department 2006). North Thailand accounts for 11 percent of Jasmine production (Luawmek 2008). Organic Jasmine rice is found in this region, providing more produce per rai and improving the soil conditions (Theerapongthanakorn & Namdang 2006). In some Western countries, it is also more acceptable.

Inputs of rice production are classified into tradable inputs, such as imported fertilizers and pesticides, and non-tradable inputs, such as land, labor, and local capital (Yao 1997). According to Sudanich (2002), inputs that were important to Thai farming were capital, labor, chemical fertilizers, pesticides, and technology such as harvest tractors. Thai farmers have incurred higher costs due to their use of pesticides and chemical fertilizers rather than using organic fertilizers. Farmers' sources of funds are Bank for Agriculture and Agricultural Co-opertives, merchant, and relatives.

The most popular rice for trading is Jasmine *Khor Kor* 105 and Sticky Rice *Khor Kor* 6 is popular for their consumption (Sudanich 2002)

Studies of farmers in Tumbol Bungngam, Tungkuawluang District, Roi-Et Province showed that growing rice in 10 rai lots provided higher yields per rai than in larger areas because farmers were able to take care of all factors related to productivity (Sudanich 2002).

Productivity of Jasmine rice in Thailand increased from 6.42 tons in 2005 to 6.49 tons in 2006. Seventy percent of Jasmine rice is exported and thirty percent is for internal consumption in 2006.

Rice Market

Marketing channels of Jasmine rice involve the domestic and foreign markets (Patthanapongpaiboon 2003). Thai farmers have several ways to sell their rice in the domestic market. They might sell their produce direct or indirectly to agricultural cooperatives, rice mills, local merchants, or middlemen. In the case of export produce, most farmers sell through rice mills, middlemen, or export companies. Few of them handle the exporting themselves. In the global market, important importers of Jasmine rice are the EU, US, Canada, Africa, and other Asian countries.

Competition

Competition in the global rice market is intense. The dominant rice exporters are Thailand, Vietnam, and India, accounting for 60 percent of global exports (Headey 2010). Thailand is the largest rice exporter even though its rice production ranks fourth behind China, India, and Vietnam (Co & Boonsarawongse 2007; Food Institution 2007). Its rice comprises around 30 percent of global exports (Headey 2010); significant competitors are Vietnam, India, and Pakistan (Co & Boonsarawongse 2007, Hansutthiwarin 2004).

Vietnam is a crucial competitor of Thailand and enjoys the advantage of low costs due to the government's support to reduce the cost of production via the provision of materials, equipment, and/or subsidized funds. Therefore, Vietnam uses price strategy to compete in the global market since its costs are lower than other rice exporters (Luawmek 2008). However, Vietnam's rice quality is lower than Thailand's.

Rice Price in the Global Market

The international rice price is influenced by demand and supply, government intervention, export volume, rice quality, slow yield growth, macroeconomic imbalance, and speculation (Headey 2010; Co & Boosarawongse 2007).

Basically, the price is determined by demand and supply in the rice market. If there is more demand than supply, the price rises. For example, Thai farmers receive a low price at the beginning of the harvest season because there is a large amount of produce in the rice market. In contrast, they prefer to sell at the end of the farming season, during July to October, because the price is higher. However, occasionally, governments intervene in the rice market. To control price fluctuations in the domestic market, governments extract surplus supply in the domestic market and may promote export. Governments may also influence the rice price in the international market by restricting exports, leading to an increase in price. It should be noted that governments sometimes restrict rice exports because of their desire to provide food security in their countries. Import surges are also important direct determinants of increases in rice price. The improvement in rice quality is another factor to increase rice price in foreign markets as importing countries often specify high quality standards for imported rice.

The rice price is also affected by other uncontrollable factors (Headey 2010). If rice production has a slowing yield growth, sometimes caused by drought, this reduces the supply of rice and increases the price in the world market. In addition, macroeconomic imbalance, such as different interest rates among countries, could cause currency depreciation in major developed countries and increase the rice price. Moreover, if the information related to the true levels of rice stocks is unreliable, speculators tend to panic buy, and this pushes up the rice price.

Government Rice Export Policy

A government's policy regarding the export of rice is an important factor in its competitive capability in the world rice market. In the past, governments pursued protectionist policies that aimed to guard their producers against international competition, correct market failure, such as surplus agricultural supply, provide food security to the poor, and raise national revenue (Choeun et al. 2006). Today, governments around the world favour freer trade policies to encourage international trade, seeking to provide the best choices to consumers, maximizing international trade, and providing food security to their own populations. These policy choices have been the rational responses to an array of political lobbying pressures from vested interest groups, including urban consumers, industrialists, and labor unions that may lead to a reduction in the social welfare of the nations (Choeun et al. 2006).

Government intervention in the rice market affects private production, prices, and market demands, and benefits exporter countries in the following ways:

1. *Production policy*. Normally, government production policies increase productivity, reduce costs, and improve rice quality to meet GAP (a standard for exporting rice, specifying production processes that are required to meet exporting standards). The Thai government provides farmers with knowledge and financial assistance to improve farmers' rice productivity and standard of product, and reduce costs. For example, money is used to train farmers and extension workers in appropriate nutrient management (Wijnhoud et al. 2003). Similarly, the Vietnamese government exempts imported inputs used to produce exports and allow farmers to exchange, transfer, lease, inherit, and mortgage land, leading to a growth in rice production, improvements in cropping intensity, and reduction in costs of production and exports (Ryan 2002). The Vietnamese government has also commenced cultivation of hybrid rice. A recent study showed that agricultural policy distortions influence rice productivity (Rakotoarisoa 2010). The study found that high levels of rice subsidies and protection in developed countries combined with taxation of rich farming in developing countries widened the gap in rice productivity between developed and developing countries. Developed countries, such as Australia, Italy, Japan, Korea, and the US, heavily subsidize their rice production and export, setting high and numerous import protections. A second group of countries consisting of China, India, Vietnam, Thailand, Pakistan, Argentina, Columbia, Egypt, Guyana, Myanmar, Suriname, and Uruguay, apply few producer subsidies, but often tax their exporters. A third group of countries, composed of mostly low income countries such as Bangladesh, Brazil, Cambodia, Guinea, Indonesia, Iran, Laos, Madagascar, Mali, Malaysia, Nepal, Nigeria, Peru, Philippines, Sri Lanka, and Tanzania, often tax their rice production and export. Rice productivity is highest in the group of developed countries, and lowest in the third group made up of low income countries.

2. *Agricultural diversification policy*. Currently, many countries support farmers to diversify their plantings to include rubber and crops suitable for making bio-fuels, leading to a reduction in the total area used for rice and rice production (Headey 2010). Rice supply in the global market reduces resulting in a price increase.

3. *Free trade policy*. The agricultural sector has lagged behind other sectors in the free trade process. Policymakers are reluctant to move

rapidly to free trade in rice because they are concerned about the stability of the domestic price and a strong demand desire for national self-sufficiency as a route to food security (Dawe 2001). Large adjustments in the price of rice can lead quickly to political instability, and governments might be more willing to accept higher levels of imports if adequate supplies of rice can be easily obtained on the international market. Dawe (2001) believes that, under free trade, domestic prices of rice were influenced by global prices and speculation of private traders and speculators. However, other studies have shown that government policies of open borders or import relaxation offer a financially inexpensive means of reducing the domestic consumption and price volatility of staple foods (Sanogoand Amadou 2010; Dorosh et al. 2009; Ryan 2002; Dorosh 2001). These studies found that private traders enjoyed the freedom to import and export agricultural products when market conditions permitted and that free trade allowed domestic markets to moderate the demand and supply of rice, and the price. If governments restricted import or closed borders, this might lead to a reduction in consumption and expensive rice in. Likewise, export restrictions could lead to a reduced supply in the world market and stimulate high prices, and finally to a food crisis (Headey 2010). Similarly, export promotions, such as removing export restrictions and export quotas, reducing export duty, subsidizing, supporting exporters to access foreign markets, completing trade negotiations, and reducing transportation costs, benefit domestic and international markets. Vietnam's easing of export quotas, reduction of export duty, relaxation of internal trade, and elimination of price controls assist farm prices and poverty (Ryan 2002). In addition to Vietnam's welfare gains, the world rice market benefits from that country's relaxed policies, resulting in an increased supply of rice on the world market. In summary, reductions in import and export restrictions enhance a country's competitive capability in the world market.

4. *Internal trade policy.* A relaxation of internal restrictions, such as the movement of rice, price control, and reductions in wholesale taxation, supports free trade and a country's welfare (Ryan 2002).

5. *Government-to-government purchases.* These are conducted to support farmers and exporters and to generate revenue for the countries, and usually occur in times of surplus supplies.

6. *Rice security stock policy.* Governments need to ensure that there are adequate supplies of rice for internal consumption before selling abroad. At the same time too much should not be retained as this may

affect increases in price (Headey 2010). Appropriately sized rice stocks in domestic and world markets act as protection against panic purchases and price increases.

7. *Price stabilization policy.* Price stabilization benefits consumers, producers, and the macro-economy (Dawe 2001). Poor consumers are protected from periods of abnormally high rice prices ensuring their access to their major staple food and farmers are protected from periods of abnormally low prices. It is also a crucial policy that maintains stable conditions for private investment and growth.

In conclusion, rice production is very important to numerous Asian governments because the process involves many smallholders and the food forms a large proportion of the diets of millions of people (Headey 2010). Therefore, governments normally intervene in the rice trade through export and stock policies to protect their own people. However, such interventions drive up the price of rice on the global market.

Governments' policies regarding the export of rice are viewed as the most important factor to enhance competitive capability in the world rice market. Government interventions affect private production, price changes, market demands, and provide advantages for the exporters. Vietnam provides financial support to its farmers to compete in the world market. In Thailand, despite increased exports and rice prices on the world market, farmers do not receive benefits because of their inability to export directly. There is strong evidence that agricultural factors, such as the government policies and the prices of agricultural products, are significant in the determination of income equality in Thailand (Motonishi 2006). Choeun et al. (2006) indicate that the Thai government's reduction of rice export taxation distributed more benefits to farmers.

Theory of International Trade

International trade is defined as the exchange of products and services among countries, and is composed of exports and imports (Hill 2009). Heckscher (1919) and Ohlin (1933) stated that international trade originated from the differences in costs of production of different countries. If one country has more favorable production factors, such as capital and labor, and/or has lower production costs than another country, then the first country should have a comparative competitive advantage regarding production costs (Hill 2009). Adam Smith (1776) explained that a country that has absolute competitive advantage in producing goods through more efficiency resulting in higher quality and lower costs than other countries should be producing and exporting the product to those other countries, thus creating international trade. David Ricardo (1817) explained that each country should produce and export products that it has the most comparative advantage and import products that it has the least competitive advantage. This results in the two countries receiving mutual benefits from international trade.

Exporting

Exporting is the process by which companies produce goods and send them for sale in foreign markets (Ball et al. 2010). Exporting is classified into direct exporting and indirect exporting. Direct exporting occurs when a company contacts target markets, governments, and related people in the foreign markets itself. Exporters need to have a potential in finance, knowledge, and capability to be successful in international business, making direct exporting riskier than indirect exporting via an agency that manages the risk for the producer. Export agencies buy goods from producers at low prices to compensate for this risk and this reduces producers' profits from indirect exporting.

The above overview has provided the conceptual framework as shown in Figure 1. This conceptual framework was used as the basis of the methodology for the present study.

Figure 1: Conceptual Framework

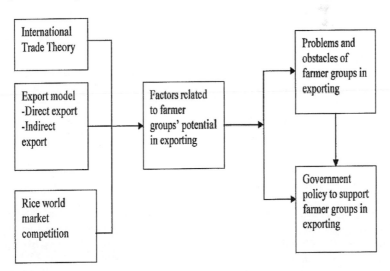

Methodology

Primary data were collected from questionnaires completed by members of farmer institutions and interviews of leaders of farmer institutions, owners of rice mills, rice exporting companies, and government officials in the Ministry of Commerce and Ministry of Agriculture. The questionnaires and interviews focused on Ubon Ratchathani farmer institutions' ability to export Jasmine rice and related government policy. Secondary data were collected from public and private organizations in Ubon Ratchathani and Bangkok, international business textbooks, and research journals. Statistical data of rice production, standards, and farmer institutions were obtained from the Ministry of Agriculture and data related to exporting from the Ministry of Commerce.

This study involved a total of 19,764 persons including farmers who were members of farmers' institutions in Ubon Ratchathani, and individuals from private organizations, such as rice mills and export companies, and government organizations related to the export of Jasmine rice in Ubon Ratchathani. The 717 farmers in this population were randomly selected by the use of the Taro Yamane formula. There were 11 district farmer leaders, 3 rice mill owners, the Director of Rice Exporting Association, Director of the Commercial Office in Ubon Ratchathani, Director of Agricultural Office in Ubon Ratchathani, Director of Cooperative Office in Ubon Ratchathani, Director of the Office of Product Development, Ministry of Agriculture, and Director of the Office of Rice Administration, Ministry of Commerce.

The study areas were Bangkok, Ubon Ratchathani and the districts in Ubon Ratchathani of Warinchamrap, Trakanpudpon, Kudkuawpun, Mungsamsip, Detudom, Buntraric, Sumrung, Piboonmungsahan, Nayia, Srimungmai, and Luasuakok. The study analyzed data qualitatively using content analysis and triangular analysis and quantitatively via percentages, frequencies, and standard deviations.

Results

Export process of farmer institutions

Most farmer institutions in Ubon Ratchathani export Jasmine rice through middlemen, rice mills, and export companies. Two farmer institutions, Development Agricultural Group and Progressive Agricultural Group, arrange their own export of rice. The Development Agricultural Group in Warin Chamrap sells their rice to an export company owned by

Wanlop Pitchpongsa, Director of Organic Agriculture of Thailand. The Progressive Agricultural Group in Trakanpudpon is the only institution that is able to complete the export itself. The leader of this group, Montri Kosonlawat, has the language skill and personal contacts with foreign businesspeople in European markets, and knows the standards required for successful exporting. His group is able to produce rice, mill and package it, and operate the export process. In summary, farmer institutions in Ubon Ratchathani export through middlemen, rice mills, and export companies. Individual farmers sell their produce to middlemen, rice mills, and government projects.

Farmer institutions' ability to export Jasmine rice

Most farmer institutions do not have the ability to export Jasmine rice because they lack knowledge in exporting, marketing, management, negotiation techniques, rice standards, producing quality rice to meet export standards, and skills in English. In addition, they do not have sufficient funds to accumulate rice and operate the export process involving buying machines and equipment to transform paddy into rice, packaging, and other expenses for export operations. Therefore, at present, farmers are rice producers only, not having the opportunity to develop their exporter skills. To export, they need to have their own quality production process, mills, packaging, customs process, and export management with foreign companies.

Factors related to farmer institutions' ability to export

The following issues were highlighted as effecting farmer institutions' ability to export rice from Thailand:
1. The institution leader needs to have ability as a professional manager. He/she should have knowledge in exporting and language skills, be able to find foreign markets, handle trade negotiations, operate the export process, and control production to achieve the group's goals.
2. Farmers have knowledge of exporting, marketing, management, and language to contribute their ability to develop the groups' export capability.
3. Farmer institutions need equipment for exporting, such as milling machines, equipment to test rice qualities, equipment to grade rice, and refining machines. These machines and equipment are expensive and most farmer institutions cannot afford them.
4. Farmers are required to produce quality rice to meet export standards. Important rice importers, such as the European market, United States, Canada, China, Hong Kong, Malaysia, Taiwan, and Singapore state

their rice standard for marketing as GAP. If farmer institutions could produce rice that meets the standards of GAP, they can sell it at a higher price. Few farmers know about these rice standards for export.

5. Farmer institutions need capital funds to operate the export process. They need funds to produce quality rice, invest in mill and export operations, and use as current capital for other important activities such as purchasing rice from farmers and accumulating supplies to meet the orders of foreign markets. The institutions need to purchase rice from farmers before they sell to middlemen. Such investments require a large amount of money.

6. A strong group network of farmers enhances their export ability. They are able to purchase a large amount of rice and accumulate supplies to fulfill export orders, increase their rice productivity and quality, have more power in marketing negotiations with middlemen, and have higher levels of operation.

7. There needs to be sincere support from government sectors, including the Ministry of Agriculture and Ministry of Commerce. The Thai government should embrace stable policies and measures to provide consistent development of farmers' ability in production and export. Also, private sectors should provide opportunity for farmer institutions to export by opening the export process and supplying information about exporting. There should be a genuine integration and distribution of benefits among stakeholders such as farmers, middlemen, rice mills, and export companies.

Problems and obstacles of farmer institutions in the export of rice

The following issues were highlighted as obstacles to the exportation of rice from Thailand:

1. Farmer institutions lack leaders who are knowledgeable and capable in exporting and professional management. They need leaders who have skills in language, and knowledge of exports and trade negotiations.

2. Farmers lack knowledge about exporting, management, language skills, global information, and capital funds in export operations.

3. Farmer associations have several weaknesses. Farmers' lack of knowledge means that they sometimes hire a manager for their associations. However, the farmers often face problems of non-professional managers, and investigations of associated matters are impracticable due to the farmers' lack of knowledge. It is becoming increasingly common that farmers' children are not willing and/or able to take over the family businesses, most preferring to work in the big cities.

4. Local entrepreneurs and leaders of farmer institutions lack confidence in exporting.

5. The government sector is not able to develop managers for farmer institutions because it cannot find persons suitably qualified.

6. Most farmers cannot produce sufficient rice to meet export standards. Major export markets, such as the European countries, Singapore, and United States, specify and accept different rice standards. This causes difficulties for the farmers because they do not know the appropriate rice standards for export or the quality of Jasmine rice. In addition to the problem of farmers lacking knowledge about the standards of rice, Thai farmers have also lowered their rice standards. In the past, Thai farmers planted rice using a natural process and equipment and harvested the rice manually. Today, they use more chemical products, technology, and machines in planting and harvesting the rice. The chemical products destroy the soil and affect the quality of the rice. Harvesting machines also cannot grade quality rice because it indiscriminately cuts ready rice and unready rice. Finally, high quality rice requires a high quality rice mill process. Therefore, producing rice of a sufficiently high standard to meet export requirements must begin with farmers and also relates to rice mills and exporters. Governments, at first, need to develop farmers to produce good quality rice.

7. Farmer institutions do not have enough productivity volume for export orders. Thus, it is difficult for groups to expand into exporting.

8. Most farmer institutions cannot access exporters through the many middlemen between them and exporters. Only big export companies approach farmers, leaving many to try to access exporters directly in the search for more benefits from rice exporting.

9. Most farmer institutions cannot access Ministry of Commerce, limiting their opportunities to receive knowledge and benefits from the Ministry's work.

10. Farmer institutions do not receive sincere support from government and private sectors. The government does not have stable policies for farmers and lacks integrated works among government's units. Private sectors often set up obstacles to farmers' access to the export process and cover important information such as rice prices. Generally, private organizations, including export companies, shipping companies, and middlemen, work together for their own benefits.

11. Groups and networks of farmers are not strong. Members often withdraw from their groups for personal reasons and benefits. Farmers might quickly sell rice to middlemen, rather than to their group, to solve problems of personal debt and may receive a better price offering

from the middlemen. In addition, farmers prefer chemical farming to organic farming because of the effort in the latter.

The above obstacles indicate that farmers will not be directly involved in export, but will instead continue to play the role of rice producers.

Government policy

There are a number of important polices of the Thai government aimed to support stakeholders in export businesses. These include:

1. *Revenue insurance project*. The Thai government created this project in 2009 to solve problems experienced by a previous scheme, the rice deposit project. Through the revenue insurance project, farmers can receive a guaranteed rice price based on the government's announced price. If the market price differs from the announced price, farmers receive compensation for the difference in prices. Farmers are required to register with the government's units and specify a period of insurance. The revenue insurance project benefits all stakeholders, especially farmers as all registered farmers receive a guaranteed and fair price for their rice. In contrast, the rice deposit project did not cover all farmers, some selling their rice to middlemen because they were not able to afford transportation costs involved in the delivery of their rice to specified places. The revenue insurance project does not require farmers to deliver their rice to specified places and they receive compensation as soon as there is difference between the announced and market prices. Also, the revenue insurance project allows middlemen, rice mills, and export companies to trade rice at the market price regularly so that they can receive normal profits.

2. *Road show project*. The government operates the road show project to introduce rice mills and exporters to foreign exporters and helping them in trade negotiations.

3. *Reduction of export and import restrictions*. Thailand has for several years removed export restrictions to support free trade. One of the measures involves the removal of export duty for rice exporters, benefitting all stakeholders. In contrast, the existence of export duties usually means that the export companies pass this cost onto rice mills, middlemen, and farmers, the last group being the poorest with little power. The government has also removed and/or reduced some tariffs and non-tariffs for rice import. These measures allow the government to increase its rice stock, exporters to be able to sell more rice, and Thai consumers to have more choice in the domestic market. However, these measures create more competition in the domestic market,

affecting the benefits of the middlemen and rice mills. It should be noted that this competition might affect exporters if some traders import rice into Thailand at low costs and export the rice to foreign markets at a lower price than Thai rice.

4. *Price stabilization.* The Thai government pursues price stabilization to control price in the domestic market. This policy benefits consumers, farmers, and the Thailand economy. Generally, the government controls the internal supply of rice and international trade volume. If there is an over-supply in the domestic market, the government extracts some from the market. To control international trade volume, the government might use export quotas or tariffs. In addition, the revenue insurance is another project to stabilize the price of Thai rice.

5. *Rice stock policy.* The Thai government maintains levels of rice stock to ensure that Thai consumers have enough rice to consume. Surplus rice is allowed to be exported to foreign markets. This benefits consumers' and farmers' welfare. The rice stock policy is parallel to the price stabilization policy, ensuring the rice price and security of consumption for farmers.

Thailand's difficulties in exporting Jasmine rice

Thailand is faced with a number of problems in the export of Jasmine rice. These include:

1. Increased numbers of Jasmine rice producers in the world rice market, such as Vietnam, Cambodia, and China. China has announced, for example, that it will produce enough Jasmine rice in 3 to 5 years to allow it to stop imports from Thailand.

2. Thailand's policymakers and marketing makers are not integrated in their operations, affecting the efficiency of the operation of exports.

3. Thailand often has problems of inconsistency of policies. Changes in government often result in changes of rice policy.

4. Thailand has difficulty in improving the quality of rice export.

5. Traders in the foreign markets mix artificial Jasmine rice with the Thai Jasmine rice product, and then sell it on international markets. This ruins the reputation of Thai Jasmine rice, causing confusion for buyers and affecting future developments.

Discussion and Conclusions

This research provides similar and different results to previous studies. Similar to Patthanapongpaiboon's study (2003), marketing channels of Thai farmers involve the domestic and foreign markets. In addition, there are similarities in farmers' exporting process. The present study also demonstrates similar problems of farmers about production costs and marketing to the studies of Sudanich (2002) and Patthanapongpaiboon (2003). The Thai government subsidized policies of rice production and exporting are mentioned in this study and the study of Wijnhoud et al. (2003). Furthermore, this study shows similar result to Luawmek's (2008) that Vietnam has a comparative advantage of rice price in the global market.

Different results adding to existing evidence of farmers' exporting process and exporting capability are Ubon Rachathani farmer groups' ability in exporting Jasmine rice as a statistical number, factors related to Ubon Ratchathani farmer groups' ability in exporting, problems of Ubon Ratchathani farmers in exporting jasmine rice in details of many aspects. In addition, this study reveals in details how government policies and projects support farmers and other stakeholders to export the rice.

The findings indicate that a major policy of the Thai government, the 'revenue insurance project', benefits all stakeholders, especially farmers. However, other government policies have weaknesses; for example, the production and export policies. The Thai government has not integrated related sectors to assist farmers and cannot solve problems of high cost and debts due to their production improvement. This has made Thai exports less competitive in terms of costs compared to Vietnam.

The Thai government's policy about free trade supports exporters and other stakeholders, but not farmers. Policies that remove export duties, subsidies, and trade shows also assist other groups, but fail to help farmers. There is a clear need to introduce policies and measures to assist farmers as well as other groups.

The rice security stock policy of the Thai government is admirable because it maintains a good level of stock to secure internal consumption and controls the stock compatible with assistance for farmers by extracting surplus rice from the domestic market.

Similarly, the price stabilization policy of the Thai government is also good as it allows the government to intervene to assist consumers, farmers, and the economy. However, in the future of Asian free trade, the government might have to rethink its balance between importing rice and rice stocking. Under the free trade condition, even though Thailand is the biggest rice exporter who has enough rice to consume in domestic market, it needs to allow rice importing into its domestic market.

The rice industry has long been a critical player in the Thai economy (Choeun et al. 2006). It provides the main staple food, employs a large portion of the labor force, and contributes revenue and foreign exchange earnings to the government. Thai rice exports have grown continually. However, Thai farmers have not always received the economic benefits from the export of rice and their earning growth is not compatible to export growth and rice price increases. The Thai government has created some good policies, nevertheless, there are some weaknesses and incomplete issued are needed to be addressed.

Recommendations

The Thai government has made efforts to develop farmers' knowledge in the improvement of rice productivity. However, integration of different government sectors is required to further enhance farmers' productivity and quality. This would support Thailand's comparative advantage to compete in the world market in term of quality rice in short term and compete with the price strategy in the long term.

The government's actions to distribute benefits to stakeholders, especially farmers, should be performed as equally as possible. There is a need for private sector involvement in exports, price control, marketing assistance, information perfection, and stable policy.

The Thai government's road show projects for exporters and rice mills are helpful but they need to be extended to support farmers. In addition, the government should provide farmers with access to financial sources and information sources on price, food production, international markets, and public and private sector marketing systems.

Another important policy is the price stabilization policy. The Thai government as a rice exporter should pursue this policy continually. Price control is necessary to control demand and supply of rice in the domestic market. Major measures to stabilize prices control the quantity of international trade and quotas or tariffs (Dawe 2001).

Furthermore, the government should find a balance between free trade and price stabilization. Thailand needs to import rice in the era of Asian free trade so the government needs to carefully determine the rice stock and conduct appropriate measures to stabilize the rice price. Effects on stakeholders are important factors for the government to consider.

Finally, the government should also provide a stable and credible policy for stakeholders in rice exporting and assist farmers and other stakeholders continually.

It is suggested that future research related to this area of study should involve pilot projects in Ubon Ratchathani to promote some areas for rice exporting. This may include groups of farmers who produce large quantities of rice and wish to be involved in direct exporting. Other research could investigate and assess government policy in exporting Jasmine rice.

References

Ball, G., Geringer, M., Minor, M. and Mcnett, J. 2010. *International Business: The Challenge of Global Competition*. New York: McGraw-Hill Irwin

Co, H.C. & Boonsarawongse, R. 2007. Forecasting Thailand's rice export: Statistical techniques vs. artificial neural networks. *Computers & Industrial Engineering*. 53:610-627

Choeun, H., Godo, Y. & Hayami, Y. 2006. The economics and politics of rice export taxation in Thailand: A historical simulation analysis, 1950-1985. *Journal of Asian Economics*. 17:03-125

Dawe, D. 2001. How far down the path to free trade? The importance of rice price stabilization in developing Asia. *Food Policy*. 26:163-175

Dorosh, P.A. 2001. Trade Liberlization and National Food Security: Rice Trade between Bangladesh and India. *World Development*. 29(4):673-689

Dorosh, P.A., Dradri, S. & Haggblade, S. 2009. Regional trade, government policy and food security: Recent evidence from Zambia. *Food Policy*. 34:350-366

Hathaphanich, K. 2009. *The Export of Thai Hom Mali Rice to the People's Republic of China*. Unpublished Masters dissertation. Bangkpok: Ramkhamhaeng University

Headey, D. 2010. Rethinking the global food crisis: The role of trade shocks. Food Policy. 35: 250-267

Hill, C.W. 2009. *International Business: Competing in the Global Marketplace*. New York: McGraw-Hill Irwin

Luawmek, K. 2008. *The Export of Thai Jasmine Rice to the United States of America*. Unpublished Masters dissertation. Bangkok: Ramkhamhaeng University

Motonishi, T. 2006. Why has income inequality in Thailand increased? An analysis using surveys from 1975 to 1998. *Japan and the World Economy*. 18:464-487

Pattanapongpaibul, K. 2009. *The Export of Thai Hom Mali Rice in the World Market*. Unpublished Masters dissertation. Bangkok: Ramkhamhaeng University

Rakotoarisoa, M.A. 2010. The impact of agricultural policy distortions on the productivity gap: Evidence from rice production. *Food Policy*. 35

Ryan, J. 2002. Assessing the impact of food policy research: rice trade policies in Vietnam. *Food Policy.* 27:1-29

Sanogo, I. & Amadou, M.M. 2010. Rice market integration and food security in Nepal: The role of cross-border trade with India. *Food Policy.* 35:312-322

Sudanich, W. 2002. *Rice Trade of Thai farmers: A Case Study of Farmers in Shee River Area, Tumbon Bungngam, Tungkuawlung Subdistrict, Roiet Province.* Unpublished Masters dissertation. Roi Et: Roiet Rajjapat University

Theerapongthanakorn, S. & Namdang, N. 2006. *The Possibility of Hom Mali Rice production in organic Farming Systems as an Alternative to Farming Career with Poverty Alleviation Potential for Lower-Northeastern Farmers.* Ubonrachathani: Ubonrachathani University

Wijnhoud, J.D., Konboon, Y. & Lefroy, R.D.B. 2003. Nutrient budgets: Sustainability assessment of rainfed lowland rice-based systems in northeast Thailand. *Agriculture, Ecosystems and Environment.* 100:119-127

Yao, S. 1997. Rice production in Thailand seen through a policy analysis matrix. *Food Policy.* 22(6):547-560

CHAPTER TEN

FEMININE WORK ETHIC IN SMALL BUSINESS: WOMEN SMALL BUSINESS OWNERS IN THAILAND'S *KUAN IM* MOVEMENT

JITNISA ROENJUN AND MARK SPEECE

Abstract

This paper presents pilot qualitative work among women small business owners who follow Kuan Im Bodhisattva in urban Bangkok. Kuan Im's following can be seen as part of the broader Buddhist reform movement in urban middle class Thailand, which is fostering improved ethics, including especially in business. The in-depth interviews were conducted by a former small business owner, who is also a follower of Kuan Im. Here, we specifically examine how religiosity of small business owners influences recruitment and training. Kuan Im serves as a role model, teaching that women can do anything men can do. This translates into policies oriented toward hiring and developing women employees.

Introduction

During the past two decades, Thailand's urban middle class has become increasingly disenchanted with the results of modern development. Many middle class Thai have come to the view that economic success has not bred happiness; but rather, new and bigger problems on many fronts. They are turning to Buddhism for guidance in dealing with problems in personal and public life. However, many feel that traditional official institutional Buddhism is incapable of meeting modern needs; "Middle class people are very different from the rural Thai villagers who had been the major followers of traditional Thai Buddhism" (Satha-Anand 1990, p.396).

Baker and Phongpaichit (2005) talk about such things as the need to find new ways to practice Buddhism when people are no longer embedded in their local communities, greater sophistication of the increasingly educated populace, and the development of a 'religious market place' as consumer culture and modern communication methods became increasingly prevalent. Traditional Buddhism seems somewhat irrelevant, focused on the traditional dichotomy between the Thai elite and the rural masses, and unable to address modern problems. Phra Payutto summarizes the issue well:

> "when the modernists began to be disillusioned and dissatisfied with modernization [they] turned to find meaning and answers from [Buddhist] tradition. However, as the traditionalists have long been far removed from the real world of changing values, they cannot supply the answers or satisfy the need of the modernists" (Payutto 2007, p.56).

Thus, they have turned to various versions of reform Buddhism. The three most commonly discussed movements strongly agree on the need for personal morality, including, importantly, in business. It has long been argued that religiosity can foster business ethics (see, for example, Sauser 2005), although some observers see "little empirical support…to demonstrate the actual influence of religion on individual decision making" (Middelstaedt 2002, p.11). However, in Buddhist contexts, at least, there is some evidence showing the positive impact of personal ethics. One possible reason for this may be the strong emphasis on individual responsibility in Buddhism (Brammer 2007). Many small business owners in these Thai movements take business ethics very seriously (Horayangura 2007).

The growing popularity of the Bodhisattva *Kuan Im* (Chinese *Kwan Yin*) can be seen as a fourth stream in this broad movement. *Kuan Im* seems to be an adaptation of traditional popular Buddhism to modern, urban middle class life, rather than an attempt to purge Buddhism of so-called 'irrational' popular elements, as in many of the movements (Ganjanapan 2003). However, little empirical work actually examines this movement in much detail, particularly in a small business context. We found that *Kuan Im*'s followers do indeed fit the profile of urban middle class Thai who are uneasy about the modern situation, and want, in particular, better business ethics. We also found that among many women small business owners, *Kuan Im* is a sort of role model for the independent woman who can succeed and provide ethical guidance for women employees to succeed.

The *Kuan Im* Movement as Reform Buddhism

Three of these reform movements have received considerable scholarly attention: Buddhadāsa-type, Wat Dhammakāya, and Santi Asoke ('Buddhadāsa-type' being used here as shorthand to represent a somewhat broader set of views than only those of Buddhadāsa Bhikkhu). "These three movements all make serious attempts to communicate and to answer the spiritual needs of the Thai people, particularly the urban middle class in the modern context" (Satha-Anand 1990, p.397).

Satha-Anand uses the three divisions of the Eightfold Path (*sīla, samādhi,* and *paññā;* i.e., moral discipline, mental discipline, and wisdom; Harvey 2000, p.37) to summarize key characteristics of the directions these movements have taken, calling them "the *sila* group (Santi Asoke), the *samadhi* group (Dhammakaya) and the *panya* group (Buddhadasa)" (Satha-Anand 1990, p.405). This, of course, over-simplifies; in fact, they all take more rigorous ethics into middle class lay society, not restricting them to the monastic community.

> "Urban professionals propose new definitions of lay ethics in modern social and political contexts that emphasize religious attainment and activism in society...The enhanced weight attached to the ethics and conduct of Buddhist lay society invokes certain Mahayana concepts and highlights the heterodox, pan-Buddhist, and ecumenical character of these new movements within a predominantly Theravada Buddhist context...The new Buddhist movements further emphasize moral discipline as the basis for social action or activism" (Schober 1995, p.209).

Kuan Im in Thailand is often discussed in terms of 'spirit cults', as a form of popular Buddhism. However, growing popularity is better understood as part of this modern urban reform Buddhism, rather than as a popular 'spirit cult'. Following the spirit of Satha-Anand's (1990) shorthand designation of *sīla, samādhi,* and *paññā* for the other three main Buddhist reform movements, we might call *Kuan Im*'s movement the '*saddhā* ' (faith) group; "Faith and spiritual strength...serve as a primary step toward further and more energetic practice of the teachings" (Payutto 2007, p.64). *Kuan Im* is solidly rooted in spiritual aspirations and a desire for a more moral life. Compared to the spirit cults of popular Buddhism, that of *Kuan Im*:

> "is more organized, in the same way as the Buddhist reform movements [Ganjanapan briefly discussed Wat Dammakaya and Santi Asoke]. Although the two types of cults [contrasting Kuan Im with other spirit cults] share the same secular concerns, Chao Mae Kuan

Im is more oriented towards the reproduction of morality in a religious sense, given the belief in the goddess is rooted in the bodhisattva concepts of Mahayana Buddhism. In this sense, the cult also incorporates the religious ethos and morality of Mahayana Buddhism, which enhances its position in the eyes of the urban middle class in comparison with the traditional spirit cults" (Ganjanapan 2003, p.131).

"[*Kuan Im*'s] wide-scale popularity among the urban Sino-Thai middle class is linked more to moral than to political or economic aspects of life as experienced by urban dwellers. By establishing some religious restrictions for its followers (observation of Buddhist basic precepts, strict vegetarianism and merit-making with monks), the cult provides moral and ethical practices for achieving success in life and solving hardships and difficulties. Guanyin is well known for her compassion and kindness and is believed to help her followers to prosper in business" (Kitiarsa 2005, p.480).

Historically, *Kuan Yin* has usually played a very similar role in China, appealing to people who place faith in her, and hope to achieve material success in a moral manner, but are disenchanted with official religious institutions. For example, a medieval Chinese commentary on an invocation [dhāranī] to *Kuan Yin* says (Yü 2001):

"The term 'dhāranī' means to keep all virtues completely. The extended meaning of the term then is thus the keeping of all virtues. For this reason, the merit of keeping the dhāranī is indeed limitless. With this, Kuan-yin teaches people to do good. Therefore, if the practitioner does good when he chants the words of the dhāranī, blessings as numerous as the sands of the Ganges will instantly come to him. But if he does not dedicate himself to goodness, he will lose touch with the basis of the dhāranī. Even if he chants it, the benefit will be slight" (p.140)...The [*Kuan Yin*] cult was quite independent of monastic backing. One chanted the scripture in the privacy of one's home and it did not require any ritual that had to be performed by monks (p.134-135)...All of them [several manifestations of *Kuan-Yin* in Chinese history] break away from social conventions in order to teach a spiritual lesson. They compel people to question the superficial values of society so that they can find true salvation" (p.210).

Receptivity in Thailand to *Kuan Yin*, a Chinese Mahāyāna *bodhisattva*, is, of course, much broader than just among Thai-Chinese. Due to Chinese cultural influence, the wider middle class tends to hold strongly commercial values more characteristic of Chinese culture than of Thai traditional agricultural society, whether or not people are actually Thai-Chinese ethnically (Komin 1991; Speece & Igel 2000). This cultural mix and diffusion of values does build in some receptivity to Mahāyāna concepts. It is not quite as simple as complete adoption of Chinese Mahāyāna; rather, Thai-Chinese identity is generally constructed around Thai Buddhism, but uses Confucianism and Chinese Mahāyāna regarding family and business (Stengs 2009, pp.22-23). These values have spread beyond ethnic Chinese circles:

The appeal of Sino-Thai culture for other urban Thai can partly be explained by the inclination of people longing for middle class status to adopt 'tokens' of middle class culture, which, by implication, are distinctive elements of Sino-Thai culture, in particular Sino-Thai ethics (Stengs 2009, p.23).

We might say that because Thai-Chinese are so well integrated into Thai society, pure Thai regard Thai-Chinese culture and values as simply a variation on Thai culture. Thus, pure Thai, especially urban middle class, find it easy to adopt some of these values without having to agonize about their own cultural identity, as some might if they adopted 'foreign' ideas.

Religiosity and Business Ethics among Small Business Owners

Increasingly, evidence shows that spiritual people "are prone to perceive the ethical nature of business issues more clearly and are more sensitive to corporate social performance" (McGhee & Grant 2008, p.61). "When one holds fast to such religious beliefs, then one seeks to exhibit behavior in daily life and work which conforms to them" (Sauser 2005, p.349). But, Sauser (2005) notes problems in actual implementation – sometimes the need to compete, to make profits, even to follow the boss's orders, can override personal ethics. Authority and responsibility are often diffuse in bureaucratic organizations, and the average employee cannot do very much. Under such conditions, personal ethics may not have much impact.

This seems to be less of a problem for devout Buddhists. For example, Brammer et al. (2007) used data from over 17,000 managers worldwide to assess whether respondents identifying themselves strongly with their religions did, in fact, have greater concern for corporate social responsibility compared to managers who did not strongly identify with any religion. Most of the 594 Buddhists in this sample were either Japanese or Koreans (and thus, represent Mahāyāna traditions). "Surprisingly, only Buddhists show a clear preference for ethical business behaviour compared to nonbelievers (p = 0.000)" (Brammer et al. 2007, p.235). In fact, 55 percent of Buddhist managers said they should go beyond simply the ethical standards required by law, to actively help build a better society. This was nearly 20 percent higher than any other religious group or non-religious respondents in the sample.

In another study, Sri Lankan business leaders reported applying ethical principles based on their religion (Fernando & Jackson 2006). The Buddhists in the sample (Theravāda in Sri Lanka) thought carefully about whether their decisions were in accord with the precepts; "I think within the five precepts, whether I am right or wrong. Every time I take a decision, I think within these five precepts" (quoting a Buddhist respondent, p.34). These business leaders do certainly strive to be profitable, but sometimes the 'right' thing takes priority. One could say that religion-based spirituality need not ignore profits, but subordinates profit to broadly-defined morality.

This same concern for morality is apparent among Thai managers and business owners in the few projects that have explicitly looked at the issue (Speece 2010). For example, Horayangura (2007, p.283) says that "for the spiritually inclined, the most salient consideration is not monetary remuneration, but whether a job allows for or even directly supports their spiritual practice". As they developed their understanding of Dhamma, respondents in this study became increasingly sophisticated in their views of right livelihood, thinking carefully about whether their jobs cause harm or break the precepts in any way. For example, (Horayangura 2007):

> "Daeng has developed a subtler interpretation of the precept on stealing [related to her family's textbook business]…Daeng reveals…that nowadays corruption is unavoidable when bidding for textbook contracts from government schools…It's like stealing the nation's money, money that should really have been used for the nation's development…She considers this kind of work a tainting of her precepts and has chosen not to continue it" (p.285).

> "Mi believes corruption is not only endemic to the publishing business, but the contemporary business world at large. Through her experiences working as an auditor in a large accountancy firm and the finance manager of her family's hotel, she says she has seen how it is virtually impossible to avoid under-the-table payments, circumvention of laws, or smooth-talking that involves lying in doing business" (p.286).

> "[Ko] believes businesses that sell jewelry or other luxury items are problematic because they stimulate people's desire for unnecessary things and encourage them to spend money wastefully" (p.287).

Horayangura (2007, p.288) reflects on the more devout business people moving "from 'not wrong' to 'right' livelihood"; that is, they come to believe that their work should not simply 'cause no harm', but should promote welfare in society. This is the proactive view of right livelihood espoused by many proponents of Buddhist economics, such as Phra Payutto (1994a):

> "Right Livelihood…is not determined by the amount of material wealth it produces, but rather by the well-being it generates. Many livelihoods which produce a surplus of wealth simply cater to desires rather than providing for any true need" (p.245).

There seems to be little easily accessible research on how such commitment to Buddhist values affects treatment of employees, but Prayukvong (2010) reports one study showing that devout owners of larger factories take Buddhist precepts seriously in employee relations. For example, in the view of one factory owner:

> "the high stock value of the company is not a true success indicator either. He obtains satisfaction from hearing that his employees are able to improve their house, purchase their own land or build a house which they proudly invite him to see. His factory can produce changes in people for the better. If a heavy drinker or drug addict chooses to change their lifestyle that is a profit he values" (Prayukvong 2010, p.10).

This factory owner paid somewhat higher wages than market rate, and argued (unsuccessfully) in the Chamber of Commerce to get support for raising the legal minimum wage. He provides medical benefits, educational programs, and helped employees set up a cooperative to get better prices through bulk purchases of everyday products. On the job safety is a priority. Workers who had left and then come back reported that there were not many employers in the province who provided such good working conditions and benefits.

Methodology

The present study involves exploratory work, with an initial research methodology that might loosely be defined as ethnographic. "The ethnographer often begins with (participant) observation, which is later complemented by other data (interviews, documents)" (Eriksson & Kovalainen 2008, p.161). They note that business research usually does not completely follow traditional ethnographic research methods; notably the extended fieldwork which can last for years. However, the first author of this paper is a follower of *Kuan Im*, and goes to the *Kuan Im* temple sometimes, so takes a thoroughly 'EMIC' approach, as is usual in ethnographic research. Thus, there was substantial background knowledge (participant observation) well before ever thinking of this project (the second author follows the Buddhadāsa-type movement, and has conducted research on Buddhist economics and business ethics in the three Buddhist reform movements noted above. This provides 'ETIC' balance).

Key informants often provide much of the detailed information that comes from interviews (Eriksson & Kovalainen 2008). The three key informants noted in this paper are women shop owners who frequent *Kuan Im*'s temple in Chon Buri. Their shops are large enough to have several employees. These women key informants have seen the author often enough to recognize her as a 'participant'. This helped with access among the key informants, consistent with a recommendation about judgment sampling in Srijumpa et al. (2004). Continuing the qualitative work will likewise take advice from Srijumpa et al. (2004) by following a chain of introductions from the initial key informants:

> "In Asia, with its strong traditions of business secrecy, judgment frequently includes an assessment of access. Working through connections and introductions is frequently the only way to gain good access at any level of companies in Asia." (p.69).

Key Informant Views

We focus here on the three key informant women who are small business owners. We are in the very early stages of this research, and although we have some additional interviews, the others are either men and/or managers who do not own their own small business, so they are not included here. We do note, however, that their views are not much different from those reported here, except that men may not take quite as strong a position on the superiority of women employees. Several key themes came out in the initial interviews:
1. The shop owners are proactive in their views of 'right livelihood', and do not believe business is incompatible with right livelihood;
2. The owners aim for good working conditions and a good relationship with employees;
3. They believe that mindfulness of *Kuan Im* inspires both diligence and ethical behaviour;
4. Owners mentor employees spiritually and commercially, teaching about *Kuan Im* and training about business operations;
5. They believe that all of this is worthy of merit in Buddhism, and thus will result in good results, both commercially and in terms of spiritual development; and,

6. *Kuan Im*'s tie-in with feminist views is very apparent. Kuan Im is a role model for women, teaching that women can do anything men can do.

All of this, other than the feminist thinking that was very prominent, seems consistent with practice in the context of the other Buddhist reform movements in Thailand.

Proactive 'right livelihood', as described above among devout business people in some of the other Buddhist reform movements, seems strong among devout followers of *Kuan Im* as well. For example, the woman owner of two mini-marts believes people need to contribute something socially as well as make money in business, the same as *Kuan Im* historically helped people. She tries not to mark prices up too high, so that she can make a reasonable living but offer cheap products to customers to help them watch their budgets (the local independent mini-marts, which are not part of any franchise, tend not to be located in the more upscale areas of Bangkok).

Another woman shop owner said that she worked for a long time and advanced, she knows about how difficult it is to work hard and ethically all the time, but it helps make one's own future good and it helps make the world better. This belief that ethical work and ethical conduct of business is broadly beneficial to society has also been reported in other case studies (Horayangura 2007; Prayukvong 2010), and is characteristic of at least two of the other Buddhist reform movements noted above. Santi Asoke may dissent on the private business aspect.

The belief that ethical business practice it is also personally beneficial, both spiritually and economically, is also common among business people in the other movements. The mini-mart owner explicitly said that *Kuan Im* makes her believe that if she does good for customers, customers want to do good for her, and will connect again (i.e., customer loyalty), and this makes the business a success. This sort of specific application of the concept of karma, learned through *Kuan Im*, seems to foster a sense of what Westerner marketing managers might call relationship marketing in the context of small retailers (Adjei et al. 2009).

Responsibility for employees is very apparent; owners/managers must watch out for their welfare, and not treat employees simply as resources to be used in running the business. One shop owner reported seeing a broader lesson in her personal moral practices. She said that *Kuan Im* does not eat beef, but this means more broadly, do not eat big animals. Even more broadly, this point is simply symbolic of how to treat other beings. The lesson translates into the same thing as avoiding anything that would affect employees' lives negatively.

Mentoring, both spiritually and in terms of career development, is an important aspect of how these key informants treat employees. All three owners said that they teach the staff about *Kuan Im*. Taking time to teach Buddhism and engage in common elements of Buddhist practice is reported by others who have done research on devout owners (Prayukvong 2010). For example, one of our key informants talked about how the *Kuan Im* image in the shop encourages employees to be mindful, to work hard and ethically for a good future. If they work well (in both the diligent and ethical senses), feedback is good, too, both in terms of career advancement, and accumulation of merit for beneficial kamma.

The other shop owner observed that the *Kuan Im* Bodhisattva has worked very hard for a very long time to teach people about Buddhism to make them believe. This has benefited many people. She tells the employees that if they want go up high in work life, they have got to be ethical, and not make trouble for others, but help them. This stress on how personal morality brings material and spiritual benefits is common throughout the different strands of the Buddhist reform movement (Santi Asoke may downplay the aspect of material benefit, believing in substantially more austerity than the others, but would not disagree on the karmic impact).

The same concept noted above, about personal benefit from ethical practice, applies to treatment of employees – the three key informants all talked about some version of treating employees well, because then they will work harder, be more loyal, and help the business prosper. This, of course, requires more than just spirituality, so the shop owners teach the employees how to do the business, gradually increasing their responsibility as they learn more. This, in turn, means that they need to pay a little higher than the market rate for small business retail clerks, because the employees acquire more skills and have more responsibility than the normally low-skilled clerks in the market. The mini-mart owner even uses profit-sharing, not just the traditional bonus, at Chinese New Year. These favorable pay scales bring karmic benefits, because they are helping employees.

Thus, again, this specific application of the concept of karma, learned through *Kuan Im*, seems to foster an understanding of what Western managers might talk about in terms 'internal relationship marketing'. Strong, long-term employee relations are critical in being able to implement relationship marketing (Herington et al. 2009). "A company will not be successful on the external market if it has not first taken good care of its internal market – its employees" (Liljander 2000, p.161).

Feminist perspectives are very strong, in the sense that these key informants believe women are as capable as men (or, sometimes, more capable). These small business owners follow *Kuan Im* at least partly because she represents the potential for women to reach the highest achievements. *Kuan Im* is for women who can do everything. They associate *Kuan Im* particularly as a patron for women, and believe women who know *Kuan Im* work well (both diligently and ethically) and make the company more ethical, which helps it prosper. They translate their feelings about the feminine *Kuan Im* into personnel policy. Thus, these women small business owners employ only women.

For example, one owner said that women work harder than men, and also work more carefully than men. Thus, all of the staff in the shop are women. When working, the *Kuan Im* image makes them think about how to work hard for a good future – both in commercial terms, and for karma – and that women are as capable of commercial and spiritual success as men. Another shop owner also employs only women; she said that women can do all work, anything, and are smarter than men, as the example of *Kuan Im* shows. The women can keep everything in proper order in the store, and women can do the same work as well as men and are more responsible than men. The women often have more education than men at the same level, as well. The mini-mart owner said the same thing. In the world some women have to support men now, but this patriarchal hierarchy is not inherent. *Kuan Im* shows that women can do more than men; in particular, women can do successful business, not only men can do it.

In fact, these key informants generally believe that women are more responsible and more ethical than men, both of which help the small business prosper. As owners who benefit from the employees' work, they feel responsible to provide good working conditions and mentor promising employees, as noted above, but it goes somewhat beyond this. We started out viewing *Kuan Im* Bodhissatva's movement simply as simply a fourth stream of the broader Buddhist reform movement. However, historically (over the past few centuries, at least), *Kuan Yin* has often appealed particularly to women (Yü 2001). In a sense, these key informant women small business owners seem to have signed on to help *Kuan Im* in her work of helping other women improve their lives.

Conclusions

It seems clear that the rising popularity of *Kuan Im* Bodhisattva among urban, middle class Thai is part of the broader Buddhist reform movement seeking, among other things, to improve ethical standards in modern Thai life, notably in business. As do business people in the other three

movements which have gotten more research attention, Kuan Im's
followers believe in high ethical standards, and are fairly proactive in
thinking about 'right livelihood' and benefiting others as well as
themselves. It is interesting that the application of Buddhist values –
thinking of the welfare of others – seems to have led our women key
informants to thinking that is similar in essence to Western concepts of
relationship marketing and internal relationship marketing.

However, a distinctive feature among *Kuan Im* followers, at least for
these women small business owners, is the strongly feminist thinking.
However, we explicitly avoided using 'feminist' in the title of this paper,
because this is not the Western version which the term usually brings to
mind. These women have no real feminist ideology in the Western sense.
They simply know that *Kuan Im* shows that women can do anything they
want, in a highly ethical manner, and endeavors always to help others.
Thus, *Kuan Im* is their role model in their own small business careers, and
they follow *Kuan Im*'s example in helping other women advance.

But while not really Western feminist thinking, neither does this seem
to be exactly *Kuan Im*'s role in traditional Chinese culture. Yü (2001)
notes that Western feminist scholars sometimes view *Kuan Yin*'s role in
Chinese culture in terms of a feminist model for women. In fact, Yü (2001)
shows that *Kuan Yin* usually functions more to make women's lives
bearable within traditional cultural norms, than as a patron of women small
business owners. However, *Kuan Im* is not doing this for these Thai small
business owners; rather, she is a role model for the independent woman
who can succeed in business, using ethical means, and helping others
through the small business.

It is well beyond the scope of this paper to go into gender roles in Thai
culture, but we note that *Kuan Im*'s different role in Thailand might come
because strongly patriarchal values do not seem to run as deeply as in
many Asian cultures. For example, Falk (2010, p.111) notes the seeming
paradox of "strong and competent women alongside evidence of
inequalities and discrimination against women", but also says that "Thai
society is generally noted for its relatively egalitarian gender relations
compared to neighbouring countries in South and East Asia". Patana
(2004) describes the construction of patriarchal values, particularly in the
legal system, during the 18th and 19th centuries, and also mentions
elements of an underlying more matriarchal social organization. Bangkok
women have also traditionally engaged in trade, even in patriarchal
culture. While most tax collectors in early 19th century Bangkok were men,
women were assigned as tax collectors in the market because most petty
traders were women.

Whatever the reasons, *Kuan Im* is clearly a role model who shows that women can be successful small business owners. *Kuan Im* fosters the application of Buddhist values in small business, both in terms of ethical interactions with customers, and, importantly, a mentoring role for employees. The employees themselves are women because these women shop owners believe women make the most diligent, most ethical employees. Teaching them about *Kuan Im* helps the business, helps improve ethics in Thai society, generates good karma, and creates more women who will help do the same; all a very virtuous circle.

References

Adjei, M.T., Griffith, D.A. & Noble, S.M. 2009. When do relationships pay off for small retailers? Exploring targets and contexts to understand the value of relationship marketing. *Journal of Retailing.* 854:493–501

Baker, C. & Phongpaichit, P. 2005. *A History of Thailand.* Cambridge: Cambridge University

Brammer, S., Williams, G. & Zinkin, J. 2007. Religion and attitudes to corporate social responsibility in a large cross-country sample. *Journal of Business Ethics.* 71:229-243

Eriksson, P. & Kovalainen, A. 2008. *Qualitative Methods in Business Research.* Los Angeles: Sage

Falk, M.L. 2010. Feminism, Buddhism and transnational women's movements in Thailand. In M.Roces & L.Edwards (Eds.). *Women's Movements in Asia: Feminisms and Transnational Activism.* Oxon: Routledge. 110-123

Fernando, M. & Jackson, B. 2006. The influence of religion-based workplace spirituality on business leaders' decision-making: An inter-faith study. *Journal of Management and Organization.* 12(1):23-39

Ganjanapan, A. 2003. Globalization and the dynamics of culture in Thailand. In S.Yamashita & J.S.Eades (Eds.). *Globalization in Southeast Asia: Local, National, and Transnational Perspectives.* Oxford: Berghahn. 126-144

Harvey, P. 2000. *An Introduction to Buddhist Ethics: Foundations, Values and Issues.* Cambridge: Cambridge University

Herington, C., Johnson, L.W. & Scott, D. 2009. Firm–employee relationship strength-A conceptual model. *Journal of Business Research.* 62:1096–1107

Horayangura, N. 2007. Interpreting "Right Livelihood": Understanding and practice in contemporary Thailand. *Proceedings of the Third*

International Conference on Gross National Happiness. November. Thimphu, Bhutan. Retrieved 23 April 2008 from http://www.bhutanstudies.org.bt

Kitiarsa, P. 2005. Beyond syncretism: Hybridization of popular religion in contemporary Thailand. *Journal of Southeast Asian Studies.* 36(3):461-487

Komin, S. 1991. *Psychology of the Thai People: Values and Behavioral Patterns.* Bangkok: National Institute of Development Administration

Liljander, V. 2000. The importance of internal relationship marketing for external relationship success. In T.Hennig-Thurau & U.Hansen (Eds.). *Relationship Marketing: Gaining Competitive Advantage Through Consumer Satisfaction and Customer Retention.* Berlin: Springer. 161-192

McGhee, P. & Grant, P. 2008. Spirituality and ethical behavior in the workplace: Wishful thinking or authentic reality. *EJBO Electronic Journal of Business Ethics and Organization Studies.* 13(2):61-69

Mittelstaedt, J.D. 2002. A framework for understanding the relationships between religions and markets. *Journal of Macromarketing.* 22(1):6-18

Patana, S.T. 2004. Gender relations in Thai society: A historical perspective. In S.Satha-Anand (Ed.). *Women's Studies in Thailand: Power, Knowledge and Justice.* Seoul: Ewha Woman's University. 37-84

Payutto, Ven. P.A. 1994. *Buddhist Economics: A Middle Way for the Market Place* (translated by Dhammavijaya and Bruce Evans). Bangkok: Buddhadhamma Foundation. Retrieved February 2, 2009 from http://www.urbandharma.org

—. 2007. *Vision of the Dhamma: A Collection of Buddhist Writings in English.* Nakhon Pathom: Wat Nyanavesakavan. Retrieved February 12, 2009 from http://www.culture.go.th

Prayukvong, W. 2010. A Buddhist economic approach to a business firm: a case study. *Proceedings of the Sixth National Conference of Economists* Ramkhamhaeng University, Bangkok, Thailand. Retrieved April 6, 2009 from http://www.eco.ru.ac.th

Satha-Anand, S. 1990. Religious movements in contemporary Thailand: Buddhist struggles for modern relevance. *Asian Survey.* 30(4):395-408

Sauser, W.I. 2005. Ethics in business: Answering the call. *Journal of Business Ethics.* 58:345–357

Schober, J. 1995. The Theravada Buddhist engagement with modernity in Southeast Asia: Whither the social paradigm of the Galactic Polity? *Journal of Southeast Asian Studies.* 26:307-325

Speece, M. 2010. *Buddhist Economics and Business Ethics in Thailand's Modern Urban Buddhist Reform Movements.* Unpublished Masters dissertation. Sunderland: University of Sunderland

Speece, M. & Igel, B. 2000. Ethnic change in marketing channels: Chinese middlemen in Thailand. *Journal of Asian Business.* 16(1):15-40

Srijumpa, R., Larpsiri, R. & Speece, M. 2004. Qualitative exploratory research on customer acceptance of technology in financial services. In R.D.Sharma & H.Chahal (Eds.). *Research Methodology in Commerce and Management.* New Delhi: Anmol. 60-86

Stengs, I. 2009. *Worshipping the Great Moderniser: King Chulalongkorn, Patron Saint of the Thai Middle Class.* Singapore: National University of Singapore

Yü, C.F. 2001. *Kuan-yin: The Chinese Transformation of Avalokiteśvara.* New York: Columbia University